THE ULTIMATE SURVIVAL GUIDE

The Prepper Bible You Need to Master Survival Skills, Food Prep, and Critical How-To

THIS IS YOUR CALL OF READINESS

Picture yourself waking in the dead of night as a howling wind tears through your quiet neighborhood street, its mournful wail echoing the chaos that has gripped the world. Across the road, power lines dangle like lifeless serpents, and your once-bustling town is now eerily silent, abandoned to the creeping shadows. Your heart pounds in your chest, each beat a stark reminder that, in a world turned upside down, survival is no longer a given… but a hard-fought battle.

Welcome to the realm of the prepared, where every day is a test of resilience and resourcefulness. This is not just a story of survival; it is a testament to the human spirit's indomitable will to thrive in the face of adversity. The age of complacency is over. Natural disasters, economic collapse, pandemics, and civil unrest—these are no longer mere headlines but pressing realities that demand action and foresight.

In this book, we will embark on a journey into the heart of preparedness, unveiling the secrets of those who refuse to be victims of circumstance. From the depths of the forest to the heart of the city, we will explore the strategies, tools, and mindset needed to face the unknown with confidence and courage.

Imagine a world where the grid fails, where society's thin veneer crumbles, and where the only constant is uncertainty. This is not a dystopian fantasy but a potential tomorrow. But fear not, for within these pages lies the knowledge and inspiration to transform anxiety into action, fear into fortitude. You will learn how to stockpile essentials, master critical survival skills, and forge a community of like-minded individuals ready to stand strong together.

As you turn the pages, you will discover that survival is not just about hoarding supplies or building bunkers; it is about cultivating a mindset of adaptability and resilience. This is your invitation to step into a world where preparedness is not just a necessity but a way of life. Are you ready to embrace the challenge, to arm yourself with the knowledge and skills that could one day save your life and the lives of those you hold dear? The time to prepare is now, for the future belongs to those who dare to be ready.

Welcome to the beginning of your journey. Welcome to the path of the prepper.

TABLE OF CONTENTS

PART ONE

PREPPING FOR DISASTERS

CHAPTER 1

WHY BECOME A PREPPER?

Preparing for a disaster is one of the smartest decisions you can make for the safety and well-being of your loved ones. It's not just about having a few extra supplies—it's about gaining the confidence and peace of mind that comes from knowing you're ready for whatever life throws your way. Natural disasters like earthquakes, hurricanes, and floods can strike without warning, while power outages, pandemics, or civil unrest can upend your daily routine in an instant. Prepping allows you to face these events with a clear plan, ensuring you have the right tools, knowledge, and resources to keep your family safe and secure. It's about taking control of your circumstances and being prepared for any eventuality.

Prepping is also about achieving independence and self-sufficiency. In a crisis, public services and infrastructure may be unavailable, but when you're prepared, you won't be reliant on others for food, water, or medical needs. By stockpiling essential items and honing critical survival skills, you can maintain a sense of normalcy even during chaotic times. And remember, you're not alone in this. There's a whole community of preppers out there, ready to share their knowledge and support. This gives you the confidence to navigate any situation with ease.

Financial resilience is another key benefit of prepping. Disasters can cause significant financial strain, from property damage to skyrocketing prices for necessities. Having supplies on hand before a crisis hits saves you money, reduces stress, and allows you to focus on what really matters—protecting your family.

When disaster strikes, preparation makes all the difference. With a well-thought-out plan and supplies in place, you can act quickly, evacuate safely, or administer first aid without hesitation. This ability to respond rapidly minimizes panic and confusion, allowing you to make the best possible decisions for your family's safety. It also opens up opportunities to support and be supported by your community, reinforcing the importance of collective action in times of crisis.

Finally, prepping offers peace of mind. Knowing you're ready for the unexpected helps reduce anxiety and empowers you to face life's challenges confidently. Whether adapting to the increasing frequency of extreme weather or simply being more self-reliant, prepping ensures you're always a step ahead, ready to protect what matters most. Knowing that you've done everything you can to keep your loved ones safe is a source of relief.

Why You Must Prepare

Protect Your Loved Ones

Your family's safety and well-being rest in your hands. Picture a natural disaster—hurricane, earthquake, flood—bearing down with little warning. Without preparation, your loved ones could be at the mercy of the elements, facing hunger, cold, and danger. Prepping ensures they have food, water, warmth, and security when needed. Your foresight could be the difference between survival and suffering.

Ensure Self-Reliance and Independence

In a disaster, public services can collapse, leaving you without electricity, water, or emergency help. But what if you couldn't rely on anyone but yourself? By stockpiling essentials like food, water, medical supplies, and tools, you empower yourself to handle crises with confidence. This self-reliance means you won't be left waiting in vain for help that may not come, and you can navigate challenges calmly and calmly, knowing you have the power to protect your loved ones.

Financial Stability

Disasters drive prices through the roof as demand soars and supplies dwindle. If you've prepared beforehand, you can avoid the financial strain of buying overpriced essentials during a crisis. Stockpiling now protects your wallet later, allowing you to keep your savings intact and avoid debt when every dollar counts.

Rapid and Effective Response

When disaster strikes, every second matters. You can act swiftly and decisively with a solid emergency plan and supplies at the ready. Whether you're evacuating, administering first aid, or securing your home, your preparedness ensures that you can respond effectively, minimizing risk and safeguarding your family.

Peace of Mind

One of the most potent benefits of preparedness is the peace of mind it brings. Knowing you have a plan and the supplies to execute it allows you to remain calm and focused during a crisis. This mental clarity is essential for making sound decisions and protecting your loved ones when the stakes are high.

Adapt to Environmental Changes

Climate change is reshaping our world, making natural disasters more frequent and severe. Preparing for these events isn't just wise—it's necessary. By being ready, you equip yourself to adapt to these challenges, protecting your family, home, and future from the increasing threats of a changing climate.

Support Your Community

When you're prepared, you're not just helping yourself—you're helping your community. By being self-sufficient, you free up emergency resources for those who need them most. Plus, your preparedness puts you in a position to assist others, strengthening the bonds within your community and fostering a collective resilience that benefits everyone. You're not alone in this journey; your efforts contribute to a stronger, more supportive community.

Disaster Preparedness: A Lifelong Investment

Learning to prepare for disasters teaches invaluable skills—first aid, water purification, and basic survival tactics—that go beyond emergencies. These skills empower you to face life's challenges confidently, making you more self-reliant and capable. Preparedness is not just a short-term solution, but a lifelong skill that will continue to serve you and your family in the years to come.

Disaster Preparedness: A Personal Responsibility

Building its spiritual foundation is essential for creating a personal or family survival plan. The bond you share with your family becomes the core motivation. Don't prepare efforts fueled by a deep and abiding love for them and a strong desire to protect them. Recognizing that preparing your family—physically, mentally, and practically—for an uncertain future is a sacred duty, you accept the responsibility with courage, knowing that the first step, committing to their protection, is often the hardest.

Once you make that commitment, the ability to act on your decisions becomes paramount. It's not about grand gestures; it's about consistently taking small steps that keep you moving forward. As you embark on this journey, embrace gratitude for the opportunity to prepare before the need arises. This gratitude will strengthen your fortitude, helping you stay resilient when the going gets tough because every step you take counts. Faith in your abilities is essential. Believe in your capacity to handle whatever lies ahead, trusting that you can face challenges. At the same time, trust in your Maker for guidance and be humble enough to seek help when needed. A willingness to sacrifice also contributes to redirecting time, money, and energy toward long-term peace and preparedness, focusing on what truly matters.

Be ready to do whatever it takes to ensure your family's safety. This readiness, combined with charity, extends beyond your own family. Share your knowledge and skills with your extended family, neighbors, and coworkers, spreading the benefits of preparedness and fostering a supportive community. Finally, hope for a bright future. Keep your eyes on the horizon, believing in better days ahead.

Reflect on these qualities. Are you ready to embrace them and move forward? One of the most rewarding aspects of adopting a preparedness lifestyle is that, as you take steps in faith, these spiritual qualities will naturally grow stronger within you.

Preparedness isn't just about stocking up on supplies; it's about ongoing personal growth—every survival skill you master builds your confidence in handling whatever life throws your way.

You're here because you care about protecting your family, but the real question is: are you just concerned or committed? There's a vast difference between making a choice and making a commitment. Be aware that deciding to prepare is the same as taking action. Many people choose to be ready, but only those who fully commit to the plan actually make it real. Procrastination is the enemy of preparedness. It's time to turn your decision into action and bring your family's preparedness plan to life.

So, ask yourself—are you ready to commit?

CHAPTER 2

SET YOURSELF UP FOR SUCCESS

In the warm flicker of a campfire, as the scent of a perfectly crafted meal fills the air, you're reminded of the true power of food prepping for survival. Picture shelves lined with jars of home-canned vegetables, vacuum-sealed packets of dehydrated fruits, and neatly organized bags of nutrient-rich grains. Each item on those shelves was handpicked, not just to survive but to thrive in the face of uncertainty. Every jar and packet represents your foresight, self-reliance, and unwavering commitment to safeguarding what matters most. This isn't just about storing food—it's about knowing, with absolute certainty, that you can whip up a hearty stew from your stockpile or bake fresh bread without relying on modern conveniences. It's about mastery. Food prepping transforms you into the ultimate provider, capable of turning simple ingredients into gourmet survival fare.

Even in the toughest times, you're not just getting by—you're thriving. The fruits of your careful planning fuel your strength and resourcefulness. Envision the exhilarating confidence that comes with being truly prepared in a world full of uncertainty. As storm clouds loom and winds howl, you're calm, collected, and ready. You've trained for this moment. Your bug-out bag is packed with precision, your home fortified with enough supplies to face any challenge. Whether it's a sudden blackout that plunges the city into darkness, a wildfire threatening your home, or an economic crash shaking the foundations of society—you stand ready.

Your skills are sharp, your resources abundant, and your spirit unbreakable. Preparedness isn't just about avoiding disaster; it's about taking control of your destiny. You turn crises into opportunities, proving your resilience time and time again. In every looming threat, you see a chance to demonstrate your strength, protect your loved ones, and emerge even stronger. You are a beacon of adaptability, unwavering in a chaotic world.

Don't wait for disaster to come knocking before you act. Take charge now. Prepare with purpose, ensuring you are ready to face whatever challenges lie ahead with unshakable confidence. Your readiness is not about merely surviving—it's about thriving, emerging stronger, and more determined with each trial. The world may be unpredictable, but your resilience is unstoppable.

Here are some examples where having a disaster plan and supplies could significantly impact safety and well-being:

Hurricanes and Tropical Storms

During Hurricane Katrina in 2005, residents of New Orleans and surrounding areas experienced massive flooding, power outages, and destruction of homes. Those who had emergency kits, evacuation plans, and stocked supplies were better able to cope with the immediate aftermath and the prolonged recovery period.

Earthquakes

The 2010 Haiti earthquake devastated Port-au-Prince, causing significant loss of life and infrastructure collapse. Prepared individuals with emergency supplies like food, water, and first aid kits could sustain themselves while awaiting rescue and aid.

Wildfires

The 2018 Camp Fire in California destroyed the town of Paradise, causing widespread evacuation. Families with go-bags, evacuation routes, and essential documents prepared were able to leave quickly and safely, ensuring they had the necessary supplies to survive the immediate crisis.

Pandemics

The COVID-19 pandemic led to sudden lockdowns, overwhelmed healthcare systems, and shortages of essential supplies. Households with a stockpile of food, medications, and hygiene products could stay home and avoid exposure, thus reducing the strain on public services and maintaining their health.

Flooding

In 2019, severe flooding affected large parts of the Midwest United States, displacing thousands of residents. Those who had flood insurance, emergency kits, and plans for temporary housing were able to manage the crisis more effectively.

Tornadoes

The 2011 Joplin tornado in Missouri caused catastrophic damage and loss of life. Families with tornado shelters or safe rooms, along with emergency kits containing water, food, and medical supplies, had a better chance of surviving and staying safe until help arrived.

Blizzards and Extreme Cold

The 2021 Texas winter storm led to widespread power outages and water shortages. Those who had prepared with backup heat sources, water storage, and non-perishable food were able to endure the harsh conditions more comfortably.

Economic Crises

During the 2008 financial crisis, many people faced job losses and financial instability. Families with emergency savings, stockpiled food, and essential supplies were better equipped to handle the economic downturn without immediate financial hardship.

Civil Unrest

The 2020 protests and civil unrest in various parts of the United States led to disrupted services and increased safety concerns. Individuals with emergency plans, secure homes, and sufficient supplies could maintain safety and security during periods of instability.

Power Outages

In 2003, the Northeast blackout left millions without electricity for days. Those with alternative power sources (like generators), battery-operated lights, and a supply of non-perishable food and water could maintain a semblance of normalcy.

Tsunamis

The 2004 Indian Ocean tsunami affected several countries, causing massive casualties and displacement. Coastal communities with evacuation plans, early warning systems, and emergency supplies were better positioned to respond quickly and effectively.

Chemical Spills or Industrial Accidents

In 1984, the Bhopal gas tragedy in India resulted in thousands of deaths due to a toxic gas leak. Communities with emergency response plans, knowledge of how to shelter in place, and access to medical care could mitigate the effects of such industrial accidents.

Key Takeaways:

- Preparedness Reduces Impact: Having a well-thought-out plan and the necessary supplies can significantly reduce the physical and emotional toll of disasters.
- Immediate Response: Quick and informed actions can save lives and minimize damage during the initial moments of a disaster.
- Long-Term Resilience: Preparedness helps individuals and families sustain themselves during prolonged disruptions, aiding in quicker recovery and return to normalcy.

Real-Life Devastations

Over the past 50 years, the world has witnessed some of the most catastrophic disasters, each leaving a lasting mark on history. In 2004, the Indian Ocean earthquake and tsunami shook the world, causing unimaginable devastation across multiple countries. The massive undersea earthquake unleashed a series of deadly tsunamis that claimed the lives of nearly 280,000 people and displaced millions more. The sheer scale of this disaster is a haunting reminder of nature's raw power.

Similarly, the 2010 Haiti earthquake brought widespread destruction to the already vulnerable nation. With a magnitude of 7.0, it struck near Port-au-Prince, killing an estimated 160,000 people and reducing the capital city to rubble. The aftermath left the world grappling with the enormity of the humanitarian crisis.

China's Sichuan Province experienced its own nightmare in 2008 when a 7.9 magnitude earthquake hit, killing nearly 90,000 people. Thousands of children were among the victims, trapped under the rubble of poorly constructed school buildings. The tragedy highlighted the critical importance of infrastructure resilience in disaster-prone regions.

Japan faced one of its darkest days on March 11, 2011, when the Tōhoku earthquake and tsunami wreaked havoc on the northeastern coast. The 9.0 magnitude earthquake triggered a tsunami that not only claimed over 15,000 lives but also led to the catastrophic Fukushima Daiichi nuclear disaster. This event underscored the terrifying potential for a natural disaster to escalate into a complex technological crisis.

In 2008, Myanmar was devastated by Cyclone Nargis, which left a trail of destruction and despair in its wake. The cyclone claimed over 138,000 lives and left millions without shelter, food, and clean water, marking one of the deadliest natural disasters in Southeast Asia.

But it's not just natural disasters that have caused widespread suffering. The world has also endured man-made catastrophes of unimaginable scale. The Chernobyl nuclear disaster in 1986 stands as a grim testament to the dangers of nuclear energy gone wrong. The explosion and subsequent fire at the Chernobyl plant released massive amounts of radioactive material into the atmosphere, leading to severe environmental contamination and long-term health consequences for thousands.

In 1984, the Bhopal gas tragedy struck India, when a pesticide plant in Bhopal leaked deadly methyl isocyanate gas. The result was catastrophic—over 3,000 people died immediately, and hundreds of thousands more suffered from long-term health issues, making it one of the worst industrial disasters in history.

The 2011 Fukushima Daiichi nuclear disaster was another painful reminder of the dangers inherent in nuclear power. Triggered by the Tōhoku earthquake and tsunami, this disaster forced the evacuation of thousands of residents and released significant amounts of radioactive material into the environment.

The 9/11 terrorist attacks on September 11, 2001, are forever etched in the collective memory of the world. Coordinated by the extremist group al-Qaeda, these attacks on the World Trade Center in New York City and the Pentagon resulted in nearly 3,000 deaths and profound global repercussions, reshaping international security policies for decades to come.

The Rwanda Genocide in 1994 was a horrifying example of the devastating effects of ethnic violence. In just 100 days, an estimated 800,000 to 1,000,000 Tutsis and moderate Hutus were brutally murdered by extremist Hutu militias. The genocide left deep scars on Rwanda and the world, a chilling reminder of the consequences of unchecked hatred and violence.

In recent years, the impact of climate change has exacerbated the frequency and intensity of natural disasters. The 2019-2020 Australian bushfires, known as "Black Summer," were some of the most destructive in the country's history. These fires claimed 33 lives, destroyed over 3,000 homes, and killed or displaced nearly 3 billion animals, highlighting the urgent need for action on climate change.

Hurricane Katrina, which struck the Gulf Coast of the United States in 2005, was one of the deadliest hurricanes in American history. The storm caused over 1,800 deaths and led to catastrophic flooding in New Orleans, exposing the vulnerabilities in the city's levee system and sparking a national conversation about disaster preparedness and response.

These disasters, whether born of nature or human error, serve as stark reminders of the fragility of life and the importance of resilience and preparedness in the face of an uncertain future.

Home Security

Securing your home in preparation for a doomsday scenario requires a comprehensive approach that addresses physical barriers, surveillance, and self-defense measures. Here are 20 ways to enhance the security of your home now to make it easier to defend later:

Physical Barriers and Reinforcements

1. Reinforce Doors and Windows: Install solid-core doors, reinforced frames, and security bars on windows to prevent easy entry.
2. Install Deadbolt Locks: Use high-quality deadbolt locks on all exterior doors to add an extra layer of security.
3. Security Film: Apply security film to windows to prevent them from shattering easily.
4. Window Locks: Ensure all windows have secure, tamper-proof locks.
5. Peepholes and Door Cameras: Install peepholes or door cameras to identify visitors before opening the door.
6. Garage Security: Reinforce garage doors and install a security system to prevent break-ins through the garage.

Surveillance and Monitoring

7. Security Cameras: Set up a network of security cameras around your property to monitor and record activity.
8. Motion Sensor Lights: Install motion-activated lights around the exterior of your home to deter intruders.
9. Alarm System: Invest in a comprehensive alarm system that covers all entry points and alerts you to any breaches.
10. Smart Doorbell: Use a smart doorbell with a camera to monitor who is at your door and communicate remotely if needed.

Perimeter Security

11. Fencing: Erect a sturdy fence around your property to create a physical barrier against intruders.
12. Gate Security: Install locks or electronic access controls on gates to prevent unauthorized entry.
13. Thorny Plants: Plant thorny bushes or hedges around vulnerable areas to create a natural deterrent.

Self-Defense Measures

14. Safe Room: Create a safe room or fortified area in your home where you and your family can retreat during an emergency.
15. Weapon Training: Ensure you and your family members are trained in the use of any self-defense tools you possess, such as firearms or non-lethal options like pepper spray.
16. Emergency Supplies: Stock your home with essential supplies, including food, water, medical kits, and tools, to withstand a prolonged siege.

17. Fire Extinguishers: Place fire extinguishers throughout your home to quickly address any fire hazards. The master bedroom is one of the best places to store a fire extinguisher in the case of a night time fire. Having one on hand if a fire is blocking access to your children could be a life saver.

Communication and Planning

18. Emergency Communication Plan: Establish a communication plan with family members and neighbors to stay informed and coordinate during an emergency.

19. Practice Drills: Regularly conduct security drills to ensure everyone knows what to do in case of an intrusion or other threats.

20. Escape Routes: Identify and prepare multiple escape routes from your home in case evacuation becomes necessary.

By implementing these measures, you can significantly enhance the security of your home, making it a safer and more defensible space in the event of a doomsday scenario.

Imagine if the grid fails, and you didn't have electricity during a doomsday scenario. You would need to rely on alternative methods for securing your home, staying informed, and maintaining daily functions. Here are strategies to adapt your home security and overall preparedness in the absence of electricity:

Alternative Lighting

Solar-Powered Lights: Use solar-powered outdoor lights and lanterns for illumination.

Oil Lamps and Lanterns: Stock up on oil lamps and lanterns along with sufficient fuel.

Candles: Keep a supply of long-burning candles and matches.

Physical Security

Manual Locks and Bars: Ensure all doors and windows have sturdy, manual locks, and consider installing metal bars on windows.

Reinforced Entry Points: Strengthen doors with metal reinforcements and use heavy-duty, manually-operated deadbolts.

Barrier Methods: Use sandbags, wooden boards, or metal sheets to block entry points in case of imminent threat.

Communication

Battery-Powered Radio: Have a battery-operated or hand-crank radio to stay updated with news and emergency broadcasts.

Walkie-Talkies: Use walkie-talkies for communication with family members and neighbors.

Emergency Contact List: Keep a written list of important contacts and emergency numbers.

Surveillance

Manual Alarm Systems: Set up a system of bells or noise-makers that can alert you to intruders.

Guard Animals: Train dogs to alert you to strangers and potential threats.

Community Watch: Organize a neighborhood watch program for mutual security.

Power Alternatives

Generators: If possible, use a gas, propane, or solar generator for essential electrical needs.

Batteries: Stockpile batteries for flashlights, radios, and other essential devices.

Heating and Cooling

Wood Stove: Install a wood stove or fireplace for heating and cooking.

Proper Ventilation: Ensure proper ventilation if using alternative heating methods to avoid carbon monoxide buildup.

Insulation: Improve home insulation to maintain temperature without relying on HVAC systems.

Water and Sanitation

Manual Water Pump: Install a manual pump for accessing well water.

Water Storage: Store large quantities of potable water and learn water purification techniques.

Non-Electric Sanitation: Set up composting toilets or other non-electric sanitation solutions.

Cooking

Camp Stove: Use a camp stove with propane canisters for cooking.

Solar Oven: Build or buy a solar oven for cooking using sunlight.

Charcoal or Wood Grill: Have a charcoal or wood-burning grill for cooking.

Health and Medical

First Aid Training: Ensure all family members are trained in first aid and basic medical care.

Non-Electric Medical Supplies: Keep a well-stocked medical kit with manual tools and supplies.

Alternative Refrigeration: Use coolers with ice or evaporative cooling methods to preserve perishable items.

Security Drills

Regular Drills: Practice security drills without relying on electronic alerts.

Escape Plans: Develop and practice multiple evacuation routes from your home.

Document and Supply Storage

Waterproof Containers: Store important documents and supplies in waterproof and fireproof containers.

Hidden Storage: Create hidden compartments for valuables and essential supplies to prevent theft.

Livelihood and Morale

Skills Training: Learn and practice skills such as gardening, hunting, and manual tool use.

Community Building: Strengthen relationships with neighbors for mutual support and resource sharing.

By implementing these strategies, you can ensure your home remains secure, your family stays safe, and your essential needs are met even without electricity. Preparing for such scenarios involves adapting your plans and using available resources to maintain security and comfort.

The Unprepared Family

The Johnson family lived in a quiet suburban neighborhood, where the biggest concerns were school projects, weekend barbecues, and the occasional home repair. Life was predictable, comfortable, and the idea of a true catastrophe seemed like something that only happened in movies or faraway places. So when reports began circulating of an escalating global crisis—rumors of economic collapse, civil unrest, and widespread shortages—the Johnsons barely took notice.

"Shouldn't we start preparing, just in case?" Lisa, the mother, asked one evening as she browsed the latest headlines on her tablet.

"Don't worry, honey," replied Mark, her husband, with a dismissive wave. "These things always blow over. Besides, we've got enough food and supplies to last a couple of days if we need to."

The kids, Jake and Emily, echoed their dad's confidence, absorbed in their own activities, blissfully unaware of the looming storm.

But the crisis didn't blow over. As the days turned into weeks, the world around them began to unravel. The news grew more dire: markets crashed, cities descended into chaos, and essential services began to crumble. It was no longer just a story on the evening news—it was happening in their own backyard.

On a dark, tense evening, the power grid failed. The lights flickered and then went out, plunging their home into eerie silence. The reality of their situation hit them like a ton of bricks. The Johnsons gathered in the living room, the dim glow of a single flashlight casting long shadows on the walls. The battery-operated radio crackled with updates, the ominous tone of the announcer underscoring the severity of the situation.

"We should have prepared," Lisa whispered, her voice trembling with fear.

Mark tried to maintain his composure. "We'll be fine," he insisted, though his voice wavered. "We'll ride this out, just like we've been doing."

But as the days dragged on, their supplies dwindled. The pantry, once stocked with just enough to get through the week, now stood almost empty. The streets outside were filled with the sounds of desperation—shouts, breaking glass, the distant echo of gunfire. The world they had known was gone, replaced by a harsh and unforgiving reality.

"We need to leave," Mark said, his voice thick with dread as he looked at his family, huddled together in fear. "It's not safe here anymore."

"But where will we go?" Emily asked, her eyes wide with terror.

Mark didn't have an answer. They had no plan, no safe haven, no stockpile of essentials to sustain them. He didn't even have a weapon to protect his family. Their car, once a symbol of freedom, now sat useless in the driveway, out of gas and with no safe roads to travel. They were trapped in a nightmare of their own making.

With no other choice, they set out on foot, clutching what little they could carry. The world outside was a far cry from the peaceful suburb they had known. Streets were overrun with panic-stricken people, and every step they took was a struggle against hunger, thirst, and exhaustion.

After what felt like an eternity, they stumbled upon a makeshift refuge—a community center turned shelter, where others like them had sought safety. They were welcomed in, but the scene was grim: tired faces, hollow eyes, and the stark realization that they were all in this together, yet woefully unprepared.

As they settled into their corner of the overcrowded shelter, Lisa held her children close, her heart heavy with regret. "I can't believe we didn't take this seriously," she whispered to Mark. "We could have been so much better prepared."

Mark nodded, his face etched with guilt. "I know. We were lucky to get here safely. We need to make sure this never happens again."

CHAPTER 3

STOCKPILING ESSENTIAL SUPPLIES

Preparing for a disaster is all about being ready for the unexpected, and it starts with gathering the right supplies to keep your family safe and comfortable when emergencies strike. The good news? You might be more prepared than you think. Many essentials you need are likely already tucked away in your home. From that stash of canned goods in the pantry to the extra blankets in the closet, you've got the building blocks of a solid disaster kit. It's just a matter of organizing what you have, filling in the gaps, and ensuring everything is easily accessible. With a little effort, you can easily turn your home into a well-equipped refuge, ready to handle whatever challenges come your way.

Here's a list of 100 bare minimum items you should have to be properly prepared for any disaster:

Basic Supplies

1. Water (1 gallon per person per day for at least 3 days) for drinking, cooking, and sanitation.
2. Non-perishable food (at least a 3-day supply)
3. Manual can opener
4. Eating utensils
5. Portable stove or camping stove: For cooking if electricity or gas is unavailable.

6. Fuel for the stove: Propane or other fuels compatible with your stove.

7. First aid kit

8. Multi-tool: Versatile tool for various emergency repairs and tasks.

9. Flashlights

10. Batteries (for flashlights, radios, etc.)

11. Battery-powered or hand-crank radio

12. Solar charger or portable power bank

13. Matches or lighter

14. Fire extinguisher

15. Candles

16. Water purification tablets or filters

17. Dust masks

18. Plastic sheeting and duct tape: For sealing windows and doors against contaminants.

19. Whistle: For signaling for help.

20. Local maps to navigate your area if digital devices are unusable.

Hygiene and Sanitation

21. Moist towelettes

22. Hand sanitizer

23. Soap

24. Feminine hygiene products

25. Toilet paper

26. Garbage bags

27. Plastic ties: Useful for sealing bags and various tasks.

28. Portable toilet or bucket with a lid for emergency sanitation.

Clothing and Bedding

29. Blankets or sleeping bags

30. Warm clothing (gloves, hats, socks)

31. Rain gear

32. Sturdy shoes or boots

Tools and Equipment

33. Wrench or pliers: To turn off utilities.

34. Duct tape: Multi-purpose repair tool.

35. Scissors

36. Rope or cord: For securing items or creating shelters.

37. Shovel: For digging or clearing debris.

38. Bungee cords: For securing loads.

39. Tent: For shelter if your home is uninhabitable.

40. Tarps: For additional shelter or covering items.

Medical and Health Supplies

41. Prescription medications (at least a week's supply).

42. Over-the-counter medications: pain relievers, antacids, etc.

43. Vitamins: To maintain nutrition when food options are limited.

44. Eyeglasses/contact lenses and supplies.

45. Hearing aids and extra batteries

46. Medical supplies (syringes, blood pressure monitors, etc.)

Communication and Navigation

47. Emergency contact information: Written down in case phones are dead.

48. Copies of personal documents: Identification, insurance policies, medical records.

49. Cash and coins

50. Emergency plan: Written plan including meeting points and contacts.

51. Pen and paper: For note-taking and communication.

Comfort and Entertainment

52. Books, puzzles, or games

53. Deck of cards

54. Children's toys and activities

Baby and Pet Supplies

55. Baby formula and bottles

56. Diapers and wipes

57. Pet food and extra water

58. Leash, collar, and carrier

Miscellaneous Items

59. Emergency blankets: Lightweight, reflective blankets for warmth.

60. Ponchos

61. Glow sticks: For light without needing batteries.

62. Paracord bracelet: Wearable rope for emergencies.

63. Ziplock bags: For waterproof storage of small items.

64. Sewing kit: For minor repairs to clothing and gear.

65. Safety pins: Useful for repairs and securing items.

66. Oral care items
67. Fishing poles and tackle
68. Utility knife
69. Insect repellent
70. Zinc-based Sunscreen
71. Lip balm
72. Earplugs

Food Preparation and Preservation

73. Portable cooking stove
74. Canned meats, fruits, and vegetables
75. Long Shelf-life Dry Goods (pasta, rice, beans)
76. Powdered milk
77. Peanut butter
78. Honey: Long-lasting sweetener and antimicrobial.
79. Trail mix or nuts
80. Crackers and other long-lasting carbohydrates.
81. Instant coffee or tea
82. Hard candy for a quick energy source.
83. Comfort foods (chocolate, snacks)

Shelter and Warmth

84. Hand warmers
85. Fire extinguisher
86. Fire starter (matches, lighter, ferro rod)
87. Work gloves
88. Emergency flare or flare gun
89. Portable heater

Transportation

90. Bicycle
91. Gasoline can: For refueling vehicles or generators.
92. Spare tire and car repair kit

Financial and Legal

93. Insurance documents
94. Property deeds and titles

Additional Supplies

95. Extra Batteries

96. Solar charger

97. Portable water filter

98. Dried herbs and spices

99. Baking soda: Multi-purpose cleaner and deodorizer.

100. Vinegar: For cleaning and disinfecting.

These items can help you effectively manage a variety of emergencies, ensuring you have the essentials needed to survive and stay comfortable until normal conditions are restored. Remember to regularly check and update your supplies to ensure everything is in good condition and not expired.

THE LONG WALK HOME

The day had started like any other for Michael Reynolds. He buttoned up his crisp white shirt, slipped into his tailored suit, and laced up his shiny black dress shoes. He was ready for another day at the office, tackling financial reports and corporate meetings. Little did he know, his routine was about to be shattered.

Late in the afternoon, Michael glanced out his office window and noticed the traffic starting to build. By the time he was ready to head home, the roads had turned into a gridlock, a sea of brake lights glowing ominously in the fading light. The car radio crackled with reports of a massive accident on the main highway, and as minutes turned into an hour of sitting motionless, it became clear that Michael's usual 20-minute drive home had become an impossible journey.

"Guess I'm walking," he muttered to himself, feeling a mix of annoyance and determination. Abandoning his sedan in the fire lane, he set off in the direction of home. The air was thick with frustration, car horns blaring as drivers vented their impatience. He started walking, the smooth soles of his dress shoes clicking on the pavement with each step.

At first, the walk wasn't so bad. The cool evening air was a welcome change from the stale, air-conditioned office. He navigated through the crowded sidewalks, weaving past pedestrians and dodging the occasional cyclist. But as the miles stretched on, the novelty wore off. His feet began to protest, the hard leather of his dress shoes offering little support.

By mile three, Michael could feel the first signs of blisters forming. Each step sent a sharp pain shooting through his heels and the balls of his feet. He tried to adjust his gait, walking on the edges of his shoes to relieve the pressure, but it was no use. The blisters grew larger and more painful with every passing block.

As night fell, the streets began to empty, leaving Michael alone with his thoughts and his aching feet. He pressed on, driven by the thought of his cozy apartment and the comfort of a soft chair. But the pain was relentless, each step a battle of willpower.

By the time he reached mile seven, Michael was hobbling. His once polished shoes were now scuffed and dirty, and he could feel the blisters bursting, the raw skin rubbing painfully against the leather. He clenched his teeth and kept moving, refusing to give in to the agony.

Finally, after what felt like an eternity, he saw the familiar lights of his apartment building. Relief washed over him, giving him the strength to make the final stretch. He stumbled through the front door and collapsed into his chair, kicking off his shoes with a grimace. His feet were a mess of angry red blisters, the skin raw and bleeding in places.

Exhausted but triumphant, Michael leaned back and sighed. He had made it. The ordeal had been grueling, but he had persevered. As he propped his swollen feet up on a cushion, he couldn't help but chuckle.

From now on, he'd keep a pair of sneakers in the trunk.

CHAPTER 4
WHAT IS A BUG OUT BAG?

A bug out bag (BOB) is a portable kit that contains essential items you need to survive for at least 72 hours in case you need to evacuate quickly due to an emergency. Here's a comprehensive list of items to keep in your bug out bag:

Basic Survival Gear

Backpack: Durable and comfortable, large enough to hold all your items.

Water: At least 1 liter per person per day. Include a few bottles or a hydration bladder.

Water Filtration System such as Life Straws.

Non-Perishable Food: High-energy foods like granola bars, nuts, dried fruits, jerky, or MREs.

Multi-tool

Knife

Clothing

Extra Clothing: Including socks, underwear, and weather-appropriate layers (thermal, waterproof, etc.).

Sturdy Shoes or Boots: Suitable for walking long distances.

Hat and Gloves: For protection against the elements.

Rain Poncho: For staying dry in wet weather.

Shelter and Warmth

Emergency Blanket: Lightweight and compact, retains body heat.

Tarp or Tent: Lightweight and compact shelter option.

Sleeping Bag: Compact and appropriate for the climate.

Paracord: Useful for building shelters, repairing gear, etc.

Fire Starters: Waterproof matches, lighter, and firestarter sticks or ferro rod.

First Aid and Hygiene

First Aid Kit: Comprehensive kit with bandages, antiseptics, pain relievers, and any personal medications.

Hand Sanitizer: For hygiene.

Wet Wipes: For personal cleaning.

Toilet Paper: Compact roll or compressed toilet paper tablets.

Feminine Hygiene Products: If applicable.

Tools and Equipment

Flashlight: With extra batteries or a hand-crank flashlight.

Headlamp: For hands-free illumination.

Portable Charger: For electronic devices.

Duct Tape: For repairs and various uses.

Small Sewing Kit: For repairing clothing and gear.

Navigation and Communication

Compass: Reliable navigation tool.

Maps: Local and regional maps.

Whistle: For signaling for help.

Emergency Radio: Battery-powered or hand-crank, with NOAA weather alerts.

Documentation and Finances

Identification: Copies of personal documents (ID, passport, insurance papers).

Emergency Contacts List: Written list of important phone numbers.

Cash: Small denominations for emergencies.

Personal Protection

Pepper Spray: For self-defense.

Dust Mask: N95 or higher for protection against dust, smoke, and airborne particles.

Additional Supplies

Gloves: Work gloves for protection.

Sunglasses: Eye protection against sun and glare.

Notebook and Pen: For taking notes, leaving messages.

Fishing Kit: Basic supplies for catching fish.

Small Cooking Pot: For boiling water and cooking.

Spork or Eating Utensil: Lightweight and multi-functional.

Energy Drink Mix: To add to water for electrolyte replacement.

Trekking Poles: For stability and support while walking.

Optional Items

Small Binoculars: For scouting the area.

Local Plant and Animal Guide: For identifying edible plants and dangerous animals.

Solar Charger: For recharging electronic devices.

Goggles: Eye protection in dusty or windy conditions.

Pet Supplies (if you have pets)

Pet Food: Enough for at least 3 days.

Water: Extra for your pet.

Leash and Collar: For controlling your pet.

Pet Medications: Any required medications for your pet.

When you're on the move, it's crucial to leave some room in your bug-out bag. This foresight ensures you're prepared for any eventuality, whether it's finding critical supplies along the way or being asked to carry extra items by your family. Having that bit of extra space can make all the difference between merely surviving and thriving. It allows you to add the things you genuinely need, enhancing your sense of control and preparedness. Flexibility in what you carry could be a game-changer in a high-stakes situation, giving you the adaptability to respond to unforeseen challenges.

Strategically packing your bag is just as important as what you pack. Place the heaviest items close to your spine to minimize the strain on your back. This innovative packing method helps distribute the weight more evenly, making your load easier to carry and significantly reducing the risk of injury. Proper weight distribution can mean the difference between a manageable trek and an exhausting, painful journey when you're on the move, especially for long stretches. Keeping your core strong and your back unburdened ensures you can travel farther and faster, which could be crucial in a survival scenario.

Having your essentials easy to access is another key aspect of preparation. The items you're most likely to need in a hurry—like your first aid kit, water, or flashlight—should be within easy reach. Placing these essentials at the top of your bag, in outer pockets, or in smaller bags attached to your main pack ensures you can grab them at a moment's notice. This level of preparedness can provide a sense of security, knowing that you're ready for any situation.

If your bug-out plan includes a vehicle, keeping it ready to move at a moment's notice is vital. Ensure your car is top shape, with a full fuel tank and emergency gear prepared for weather conditions. Carry spare parts and tools for quick fixes on the go, so you're never caught off guard. But also consider having a backup mode of transport, like an inflatable boat, mountain bike, or even a skateboard, for those situations where you might need to abandon your primary vehicle. Switching quickly and efficiently could distinguish between a smooth escape and getting stuck.

If you're forced to leave your vehicle behind, knowing what to grab is critical. Be strategic about what you take with you—focus on the most critical items from your trunk, such as your bug-out bag, first aid kit, and emergency supplies, that will aid your survival as you continue on foot or switch to your secondary vehicle.

Pay attention to the small details that can significantly impact, like attaching your hiking boots to your bug-out bag. Keeping them securely attached ensures that if you need to leave in a hurry, your shoes are with you, without taking up valuable hand space. Sure, it might temporarily misbalance your bag, but you'll be ready to go once they're on your feet.

Timing your bug-out is also crucial. If social unrest, which can include riots, civil disturbances, or other situations where public safety is compromised, is part of the equation, consider moving to your bug-out location during the quiet hours—late at night or early in the morning—when both rioters and police are likely to be less active. This strategy reduces your chances of running into trouble as you leave the city.

Always be prepared for the unexpected, like crossing bodies of water. Improvised flotation devices, such as plastic bags filled with air or empty 2-gallon containers, can keep you afloat if you need to make an unplanned water crossing. And don't forget to prepare for the sun. If you live in a hot, sunny area, packing sunscreen, moisturizer, and a hat or bandanna is essential. In a bug-out scenario, long hours exposed to the sun can lead to burns and dehydration, so protect your skin to stay in top condition.

Every aspect of your bug-out plan matters, from how you pack your bag to the timing of your departure. Being prepared means thinking ahead and staying adaptable, ready to face whatever challenges come your way.

CHAPTER 5

FIRST AID

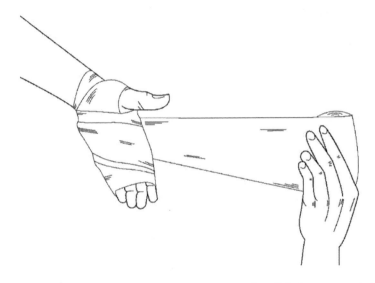

Knowing basic first aid is essential not only in everyday life but especially in a doomsday scenario when professional medical help may not be available. In our daily lives, accidents happen—a child scrapes their knee, someone at work burns themselves, or a family member cuts their hand in the kitchen. Basic first aid knowledge can mean the difference between a minor injury and a more serious complication. It's not just about reacting to an injury, but being proactive in preventing it from escalating. In a doomsday situation, where hospitals could be inaccessible and medical supplies scarce, that knowledge becomes a matter of survival.

In everyday applications, first aid skills provide a sense of security, allowing you to act quickly and efficiently when someone is injured, whether you're treating a burn, stopping a bleed, or performing CPR. This knowledge can prevent a situation from getting worse, helping the injured person until professional help arrives. These moments may seem small, but they add up to lifesaving actions that keep you and your loved ones safe and prepared for any emergency.

Now, imagine a doomsday scenario—a natural disaster, economic collapse, or widespread societal breakdown. Access to doctors, hospitals, or emergency services may be nonexistent. In these situations, knowing how to treat wounds, manage burns, or deal with broken bones is critical. Without immediate care, even a minor injury can turn dangerous, leading to infection or long-term damage. Understanding how to clean and dress a wound, perform CPR, or even stabilize a fracture could not only save lives but also prevent long-term health issues when help is hours or even days away.

Additionally, in a doomsday scenario, medical resources like antibiotics, sterile bandages, or even simple pain relievers may be hard to come by. Knowing how to improvise with available materials and understanding natural remedies can help you extend your medical supplies and keep people healthy in the long run.

Basic first aid knowledge builds resilience in both daily life and extreme situations. It gives you the confidence and ability to handle medical emergencies with calmness and efficiency, ensuring that you and your loved ones are better prepared for the unexpected—whether it's a simple accident at home or the fallout from a disaster where self-reliance is key. This preparation brings a sense of security, reducing anxiety and promoting a feeling of safety.

Treatments

Treating injuries effectively can make all the difference in an emergency, whether it's a minor issue or something more severe like a fracture or open wound. Start by assessing the injury—look for signs like swelling, deformity, or loss of function to determine the extent of the damage. Once identified, rest becomes crucial. Make sure the injured person avoids putting weight on the affected area and tries to immobilize it as much as possible.

For pain and swelling, apply ice or a cold pack wrapped in a cloth for 15-20 minutes, making sure to give breaks between applications. Compression, when appropriate, can also help, but be sure not to wrap the bandage too tightly to avoid cutting off circulation. Elevating the injured area above heart level helps reduce swelling and promotes better healing. Administer Over-the-counter pain relievers if they're available and safe for the individual.

For fractures, start by carefully assessing the injury. Look for any obvious signs like deformity, swelling, or exposed bone. Limit movement immediately and focus on immobilizing the affected area. Use a splint made from available materials like boards, rolled-up clothing, or sticks, and ensure that the splint extends beyond the joints above and below the fracture. Padding between the splint and the skin is crucial to prevent irritation or sores, and securing the splint should be done gently, ensuring circulation isn't restricted. Elevate the injured limb to minimize swelling while waiting for further medical help.

When dealing with open wounds, cleanliness is key. Always wash your hands thoroughly or use hand sanitizer before treating the wound. If available, wear disposable gloves to reduce the risk of infection further. Control bleeding by applying direct pressure with a clean cloth or bandage and elevate the wound if necessary. Once the bleeding is under control, gently clean the wound with mild soap and water, avoiding harsh disinfectants. A thin layer of antibiotic ointment can help prevent infection before covering the wound with a sterile dressing. Keep an eye on the wound for signs of infection, such as redness, warmth, or discharge.

Proper wound care is critical for preventing infections and speeding up healing. The first step is always safety, so wear disposable gloves to protect yourself and the injured person from contamination. Next, focus on controlling the bleeding by applying steady pressure to the wound using a clean cloth or bandage. Once the bleeding is under control, gently clean the wound with mild soap and water. Avoid using harsh disinfectants like hydrogen peroxide or alcohol, which can damage healthy tissue and slow down healing.

To guard against infection, apply a thin layer of antibiotic ointment over the wound and create a barrier to keep bacteria at bay while allowing the skin to repair itself. Once treated, cover the wound with a sterile dressing or bandage, ensuring it's secured in place but not too tight. Elevating the wound above heart level can help reduce swelling and promote faster recovery if the wound is on a limb.

Stay on top of wound care by changing the dressing regularly, especially if it becomes wet or dirty. Monitor for signs of infection, such as redness, swelling, warmth, or unusual discharge. If these signs appear, it's essential to seek medical attention. Keeping a close eye on the wound and giving it the proper care ensures a smooth healing process and reduces the risk of complications.

Treating a wound quickly and thoroughly can be the difference between a fast recovery and a lingering problem. Whether it's a minor cut or something more serious, the key is consistent care and vigilance.

Splinting

Knowing how to correctly splint is crucial when dealing with fractures or dislocations, as it immobilizes the injury and prevents further damage. The first step is to assess the injury—look for apparent deformities, swelling, or a loss of function. Once you've identified the injury, support the area using available materials. Padded boards, rolled-up clothing, or sturdy sticks can be splints. The key is to stabilize the injury without causing discomfort. After positioning the splint, use bandages, belts, or strips of fabric to secure it. Please ensure the splint is firm but not so tight that it cuts off circulation.

Splinting can make all the difference in minimizing pain and preventing further complications in a survival or everyday emergency. Knowing how to create a quick, effective splint from what's on hand can buy you time until you can get professional medical help or, in a worst-case scenario, serve as a long-term solution. Being able to handle such a situation reduces the risk of further injury and reassures the injured person that they're in capable hands.

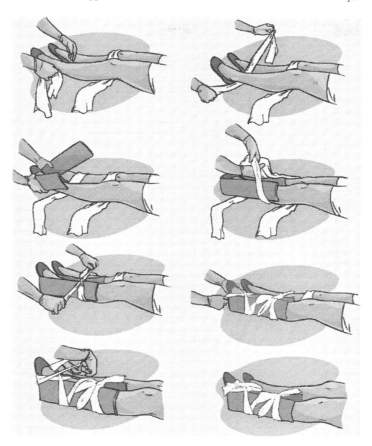

Recognizing and Treating Common Illnesses

Respiratory Infections

If someone is coughing, running a fever, or struggling to breathe, it's likely a respiratory infection. The best approach is simple: rest, hydration, and over-the-counter meds if you have them. Keep the person warm and isolated to avoid spreading the illness to others. A little care goes a long way.

Gastrointestinal Illnesses (Diarrhea and Vomiting)

Frequent diarrhea, vomiting, and stomach pain can quickly lead to dehydration. To counter this, ensure they sip clear fluids, use oral rehydration solutions (ORS), or make your own with water, salt, and sugar. Hold off on solid food until symptoms calm down.

Fever

A fever usually comes with chills and fatigue. In this case, rest and plenty of fluids are key. Over-the-counter fever reducers can help keep the person comfortable and relaxed, ensuring they ride it out with minimal discomfort.

Infection Prevention

Hygiene

Regular handwashing with soap and water is the first defense against infections. If you don't have access to water, use hand sanitizer to keep germs at bay. Keeping your environment clean can make a huge difference. Dispose of waste properly and maintain a hygienic space to stop bacteria from spreading.

Isolation and Protection

If someone in your household is ill, keep them separate from others to minimize the risk of transmission. If you have them, use gloves and masks for extra protection when caring for the sick.

Recognizing and Managing Infections

Skin Infections

It may be infected if the skin is red, swollen, and painful. Clean the area gently, apply antibiotic ointment if available, and cover it with a sterile bandage. Regularly check for signs of worsening, such as pus or increased pain.

Respiratory Infections

Rest and hydration are top priorities when someone shows signs of a respiratory infection. If over-the-counter remedies are available, use them and encourage breathing exercises to help keep the lungs clear.

Gastrointestinal Infections

Dehydration is the primary concern, so clear fluids or ORS should be offered. The individual should also avoid contaminated food and water, as these can worsen the situation.

Prevention Practices

Hydration is vital for supporting the body's natural defenses and preventing illness from escalating. Quarantining those who are sick helps protect others in close quarters, while regular handwashing is crucial for stopping the spread of germs. Proper wound care prevents infection and keeps minor cuts from becoming more significant problems. Finally, ensuring your food and water sources are clean is essential—boil or purify water when necessary.

You can effectively manage illnesses by recognizing symptoms early, applying basic treatments, and maintaining good hygiene. These simple steps can stop minor issues from becoming major health concerns, ensuring everyone stays as healthy as possible. Quick actions and proper care can make all the difference in challenging times.

Suturing

Suturing is a skill that takes time and practice to master, and when done incorrectly, it can lead to serious complications. Improper suturing can cause a life-threatening infection or result in poor wound healing, and when done imperfectly, it may still leave a noticeable scar. Medical professionals use local anesthetics to numb the area, making the process painless for the patient. In an emergency, however, you likely won't have such numbing agents on hand, which means the procedure could be quite painful. This underscores the importance of suturing as a last resort when no other options are available, and the need for professional training in this skill.

That said, knowing how to suture in an emergency can be a crucial, life-saving skill. With a calm hand, attention to cleanliness, and precision, you can handle the situation effectively. However, it's important to remember that seeking professional medical care is always the best course of action. Even if you have the knowledge and confidence to suture, it's crucial to understand that professional medical care can make all the difference in ensuring the best possible outcome.

Materials:
- Sterile suture kit (needle, sutures, forceps)
- Antiseptic solution (iodine or alcohol)
- Sterile gloves
- Sterile gauze
- Scissors (for cutting sutures)
- Tweezers or forceps
- Local anesthetic (if available) or pain relief (optional but helpful)

Step-by-Step Process for Stitching Skin

1. Prepare the Area:
First things first—wash your hands thoroughly and put on sterile gloves to prevent infection. Clean the wound using an antiseptic like iodine or alcohol to eliminate dirt and bacteria. If you have access to local anesthetic, now's the time to apply it, but if not, reassure your patient and keep calm—your confidence will help them through the discomfort.

2. Assess the Wound:
Take a moment to assess if stitches are necessary. Wounds longer than ½ inch, deep cuts exposing underlying tissue, or wounds that won't stop bleeding typically require suturing. If bleeding is excessive, apply pressure to control it before proceeding.

3. Choosing the Right Sutures:

For most skin wounds, non-absorbable sutures like nylon or silk are ideal, as they will need to be removed later. If you're dealing with deeper wounds, absorbable sutures are often used internally because they dissolve over time.

4. Position the Patient:

Make sure the patient is comfortable and the wound is easily accessible. You want the skin relaxed and flat for the best stitching results.

5. Begin Suturing:

Insert the Needle:

- Using forceps, insert the needle 1/4 inch from the wound edge, perpendicular to the skin.
- Push it through the skin and pull it out the opposite side, ensuring it emerges 1/4 inch from the wound edge.

Make the Stitch:

- Pull the suture material through, leaving a small tail on one side.
- Tie a knot by looping the thread over the needle holder or forceps and pulling it tight. Use three to four knots to secure each stitch.

Repeat:

- Continue the process every 1/4 inch along the wound, making sure the stitches are evenly spaced and properly aligned.

6. Finish and Secure:

After closing the wound, tie off the last stitch with several secure knots. Trim any excess thread using sterile scissors, leaving a small amount of suture material above the knots.

7. Dress the Wound:

Clean the area again with antiseptic and cover the wound with sterile gauze or a clean bandage. This protects the area from dirt and bacteria.

8. Monitor for Infection:

Check the wound daily for redness, swelling, warmth, or discharge—all signs of infection. Keep the area clean and dry and change the bandage regularly.

9. Suture Removal:

For non-absorbable sutures, stitches should be removed by a professional within 5-14 days, depending on the wound's location. For instance, stitches on the face may be removed after 5-7 days, while those on the body may need longer.

Tips for Successful Stitching:

- Stay calm: Confidence will keep you focused, and precision is key to proper healing.
- Proper tension: Don't pull too tightly, as this can restrict blood flow or cause puckering. The wound edges should meet without excessive pressure.
- Even spacing: Align the wound edges properly and avoid leaving gaps between stitches.

When Not to Stitch a Wound:

- Infection: Never stitch a wound that's already infected or contains debris—this can trap bacteria inside and worsen the condition.
- Animal or human bites: These wounds are prone to infection and may not always be suitable for stitching.
- Old wounds: Wounds older than 12-24 hours should only be sutured after thorough cleaning by a professional.

Encourage the person to take prescribed antibiotics if available, especially if the wound is at risk for infection. Keep the wound clean, dry, and covered for the first few days to promote healing. Always follow up with a healthcare professional to ensure proper healing.

Suturing a wound in an emergency can feel daunting, but with a calm approach and careful technique, you can successfully close a wound and prevent further complications. While this is an important skill to have in dire situations, always seek professional medical help as soon as possible to confirm that the wound is healing correctly. By knowing how to suture, you'll be ready to act when it matters most.

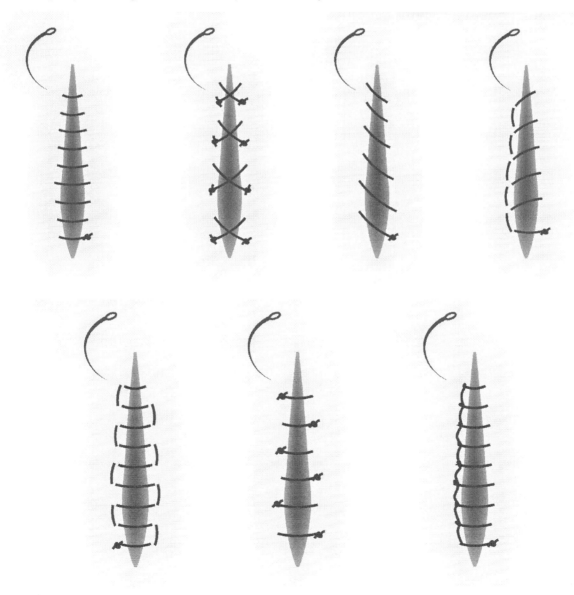

Building the Ultimate First Aid Kit

A well-stocked first aid kit is your frontline defense in any emergency, ensuring you're ready to handle anything from minor scrapes to more serious medical needs. Whether you're prepping for everyday mishaps or unexpected crises, having the right supplies on hand can make all the difference. Start with a sturdy, waterproof container—think durable backpack, plastic bin, or a dedicated first aid bag. Label it clearly so everyone knows what it is and include a list of emergency contacts and important medical details like allergies. Don't forget to regularly update an inventory list, making sure nothing is expired or missing.

Must-Have First Aid Supplies

Bandages and Dressings: Keep a variety of adhesive bandages, sterile gauze pads, adhesive tape, and elastic bandages for sprains. You never know what kind of wound you'll face, so better be prepared.

Cleaning and Disinfection: Antiseptic wipes, hydrogen peroxide, rubbing alcohol, cotton balls, tweezers, and scissors should always be in your kit. These essentials help clean wounds and prevent infections.

Medications: Stock basic pain relievers, antihistamines for allergic reactions, antacids, and any personal prescription meds. When things go sideways, having medications handy can be a lifesaver.

Tools and Instruments: Your kit should include a thermometer, CPR face shield, splints, penlight, and instant cold packs. These will help you assess and stabilize injuries like a pro.

Don't Forget a First Aid Manual: A well-organized first aid guide can be a game changer when you need to act quickly and efficiently during an emergency.

Specialized Supplies

Emergency Blankets: Great for warmth and protection when the weather turns rough or you're dealing with shock.

Burn Cream/Gel: For soothing and treating minor burns or scalds.

Eye Wash: Perfect for flushing out contaminants or debris.

Tourniquet: In extreme situations where there's severe bleeding, a tourniquet could save a life.

Scalpel: Only for those trained to use it, but handy for advanced first aid procedures.

Personal Medications and Supplies: Don't forget essentials like EpiPens, inhalers, or spare eyeglasses, tailored to your specific needs or those of your loved ones.

Extra Tips

- Storage: Keep your kit in a cool, dry spot, and out of direct sunlight.
- Routine Checks: Inspect regularly for expired or used items.
- Customization: Tailor your kit for specific needs—whether you're at home, on the go, or in the wilderness.
- Training: Taking a first aid and CPR course empowers you to use your supplies effectively.

Travel Kits

Consider creating smaller, portable kits for your car, hiking trips, or even the office, so you're always prepared wherever you are.

Building a comprehensive first aid kit is more than just an act of preparedness—it's a proactive step in safeguarding yourself and your loved ones. With the right tools and knowledge, you can tackle any emergency that comes your way, ensuring peace of mind and readiness for whatever life throws at you. Preparedness isn't just practical; it's empowering.

Triage and Medical Care in Resource-Scarce Environments

Triage is the process of quickly determining who needs urgent care, who can wait, and who, tragically, may not survive. It's the backbone of managing medical care when the system is overwhelmed, ensuring the most efficient use of limited supplies and personnel.

In a disaster or resource-scarce environment, providing medical care becomes a race against time and supplies. Triage is the key to managing these situations effectively. It's all about assessing and prioritizing patients, making sure the most critical cases get immediate attention. When resources are limited, triage ensures you're using what you have wisely to save as many lives as possible.

Triage Categories

- Immediate (Red): Life-threatening conditions like severe bleeding or blocked airways demand immediate intervention.
- Delayed (Yellow): Serious but stable injuries like fractures can wait for treatment.
- Minimal (Green): Minor injuries can be addressed later or self-treated.
- Expectant (Black): In cases where survival is unlikely, comfort care is the priority.

Triage Procedure

1. Ensure Safety: Protect both rescuers and patients before starting care.
2. Quick Assessment: Evaluate patients' airway, breathing, and circulation (the ABCs) to identify immediate threats.
3. Immediate Care: For "Immediate" cases, handle life-threatening issues like stopping bleeding or opening airways.
4. Detailed Evaluation: Once critical cases are managed, assess "Delayed" and "Minimal" patients for further care.
5. Categorize and Prioritize: Assign patients to triage categories and record your decisions for ongoing care.

Medical Care in Resource-Scarce Environments

In resource-strapped settings, you must be resourceful. It's not just about having medical supplies—it's about knowing how to stretch them effectively.

- Maximize Resources: Basic interventions, like wound care and splinting, can save lives.
- Focus on Essentials: Stopping bleeding, securing airways, and managing pain can make a huge difference with minimal resources.
- Prioritize Hygiene: Clean hands, clean wounds—keeping things sanitary is crucial to prevent infection in tight conditions.
- Clear Communication: Work closely with others, making sure everyone is on the same page about who needs help and what's available.
- Creative Solutions: Improvisation is your friend when supplies run low. Get creative with what's on hand to meet critical needs.

- Knowledge is Power: Make sure everyone on your team has basic medical skills to handle a variety of situations.

In a resource-scarce situation, triage is your compass, guiding you toward the most effective use of limited resources. By prioritizing care based on severity, using supplies wisely, and staying adaptable, you can still make a huge difference in outcomes. Preparedness, quick decision-making, and creativity are key to navigating these high-stress situations. Even when resources are stretched thin, smart triage and focused care can save lives.

THE LAST CRUMB

The sun was setting, casting long shadows over the abandoned streets. The world had plunged into chaos months ago, and in the wake of disaster, food and resources had become scarce. Emma and her two children, Sam and Lily, had been struggling to survive in their small, crumbling apartment.

Emma stood at the window, staring out at the nearly empty city, her heart heavy with despair. The pantry was bare, and the last crumb of bread had been eaten days ago. She had scoured the neighborhood, but every store had been looted, and every house ransacked weeks ago. The constant gnawing hunger was a cruel reminder of their dire situation.

I should have left with everyone else, she though miserably. But how was she to know things were going to get this bad?

"Mama, I'm hungry," Lily whispered, her voice weak.

Emma turned to see her daughter lying on the tattered sofa, her face pale and gaunt. Sam, older by only a few years, sat beside her, his eyes hollow and filled with worry. He tried to comfort his sister, but even his strength was waning.

"I know, sweetheart," Emma said, her voice cracking. "I'll find something. Just hold on a little longer."

She fought back tears as she rummaged through the kitchen cabinets once more, hoping against hope that she had missed something. But there was nothing. Every cupboard, every shelf was empty.

Desperation clawed at her heart. She had always been strong for her children, but now she felt helpless. Sinking to the floor, the weight of her failure pressed down on her. How could she protect her children if she couldn't even feed them?

A knock at the door startled her, and she quickly got up, her heart racing. She opened the door to find her neighbor, Mrs. Thompson, standing there. The elderly woman looked as worn and tired as Emma felt.

"Emma, I found a little bit of food," Mrs. Thompson said, holding out a small bag. "It's not much, but it's something."

Emma took the bag, her hands trembling. "Thank you. You don't know how much this means."

Mrs. Thompson nodded, her eyes filled with sorrow. "We're all in this together. If you need anything, just knock."

Emma closed the door and opened the bag to find a few cans of vegetables and a small loaf of bread. It was enough for a meager meal, and for a moment, she felt a flicker of hope.

She quickly prepared the food, dividing it into three small portions. As she set the plates in front of her children, she forced a smile. "Here you go, kids. Eat slowly."

Lily and Sam ate in silence, their eyes showing gratitude mixed with lingering fear. Emma watched them, her heart aching. She had managed to feed them tonight, but what about tomorrow? And the days after that?

As the night grew colder, Emma tucked her children into bed, holding them close. She whispered words of comfort, even though she wasn't sure she believed them herself. She lay awake, staring at the ceiling, praying for a miracle.

Day passed, and the little bit of food Mrs. Thompson had given them was long gone and her foraging within abandoned apartments were less than fruitful. Emma's strength was fading, and the children's cries of hunger pierced her soul. She had nothing left to give.

One morning, Emma awoke to find Sam and Lily still sleeping. Their breaths were shallow, and their faces even more gaunt. She knew the end was near, and the realization shattered her heart.

With a final, desperate resolve, she left the apartment and wandered the streets, searching for anything that could sustain her children. She knocked on barred doors, tearfully begged strangers who were better off than she for help, but the city was a wasteland, and there was no mercy to be found.

CHAPTER 6

FOOD PREPPING

Preparation is the difference between anxiety and assurance, between scrambling for resources and knowing you're ready.

Consider the peace of mind and comfort knowing you have weeks, if not months of food on hand. You won't have to worry about how you'll feed your family if the supply chain breaks down or if you face an unexpected financial hit. Your stockpile becomes a source of relief, a reminder that you've taken steps to protect those you love from hunger and hardship. It's about more than just survival; it's about preserving your well-being, maintaining your health, and staying strong when the world around you seems fragile. It's about ensuring that, no matter what happens, you have the means to sustain yourself and those who depend on you. These benefits are not just theoretical, they are real and tangible, providing reassurance and comfort in uncertain times.

So, I implore you—don't wait until it's too late. Start building your food stockpile now. It's not just about being prepared; it's about being responsible, ready, and confident that you can face whatever challenges come your way. This small effort today could make all the difference tomorrow. The time to act is now.

Preparing food for later consumption involves methods that preserve the quality, safety, and taste of the food. Here are five effective ways to prep food for later:

1. Freezing

Freezing food preserves it for an extended period by slowing down the activity of bacteria and enzymes. Foods like meats, vegetables, fruits, and prepared meals can be frozen in airtight containers or freezer bags to prevent freezer burn and maintain freshness.

2. Canning

Canning involves sealing food in airtight containers and then heating them to kill bacteria and enzymes that could cause spoilage. There are two main methods: water bath canning for high-acid foods (like fruits and pickles) and pressure canning for low-acid foods (like meats and vegetables).

3. Dehydrating

Dehydrating removes moisture from food, which inhibits the growth of bacteria, yeast, and mold. • Foods like fruits, vegetables, herbs, and meats (jerky) can be dehydrated using a dehydrator, oven, or even air drying in certain climates.

4. Vacuum Sealing

Vacuum sealing removes air from the packaging, which helps preserve food by reducing oxidation and the growth of aerobic bacteria. This method works well for a variety of foods, including meats, cheeses, vegetables, and prepared meals. It can be used in conjunction with freezing for longer storage.

5. Pickling

Pickling preserves food in an acidic solution, typically vinegar or a brine (saltwater solution), which inhibits the growth of bacteria. This method is commonly used for cucumbers (to make pickles), but can also be used for other vegetables, fruits, and even eggs. Each of these methods has its own set of benefits and is suitable for different types of foods and storage durations. Outdoor cooking offers a variety of methods to prepare meals in the open air, each with its unique set of techniques and flavors.

Canning Methods Overview:

-   Water Bath Canning: Ideal for high-acid foods (pH 4.6 or lower) such as most fruits, pickles, jams, and jellies. Fill jars with food and liquid, seal with lids and bands, submerge in boiling water, and process for the recommended time.
-   Pressure Canning: Necessary for low-acid foods (pH higher than 4.6) such as vegetables, meats, poultry, and seafood. Fill jars with food and liquid, seal with lids and bands, place in a pressure canner, and process at the specified pressure and time.

Canning food is a method of preserving it by processing and sealing it in an airtight container, which provides a shelf life typically ranging from one to five years. There are two main methods of canning: water bath canning and pressure canning. Here's how you can perform each method:

Water Bath Canning

This method is suitable for high-acid foods like fruits, jams, jellies, salsas, tomatoes (with added acid), and pickles.

Materials:

-   Canning jars with lids and bands
-   Large pot with a canning rack
-   Jar lifter and canning funnel
-   Ladle

Steps:

1. Prepare Jars:
   - Wash jars, lids, and bands in hot, soapy water. Rinse and set aside.
   - Keep jars warm until ready to use to prevent them from breaking when filled with hot food and placed in boiling water.

2. Prepare Your Recipe:
   - Cook your food according to your recipe. Typically, this involves cooking fruits or vegetables, possibly adding sugar, spices, or vinegar.

3. Fill Jars:
   - Using a funnel, fill jars with the prepared food, leaving headspace (usually 1/4 to 1/2 inch depending on the recipe).
   - Wipe the rim of the jar with a clean cloth to ensure it's free of any food particles.
   - Place the lid on the jar, then screw on the band just until it's fingertip tight.

4. Process the Jars:
   - Place jars on the rack in the pot filled with simmering water, ensuring water covers jars by 1-2 inches.
   - Bring water to a full rolling boil, then start your timer.
   - Process the jars for the time specified in your recipe, adjusting for altitude if necessary.

5. Cool Jars:
   - Remove jars using a jar lifter and place them on a towel or cooling rack, making sure they do not touch.
   - Leave jars undisturbed for 12-24 hours. Bands should not be retightened as this may interfere with the sealing process.

6. Check Seals:
   - After 24 hours, check that the lids have sealed by pressing down on the center of each lid. If the lid does not pop up and down, it is sealed.
   - Store unsealed jars in the refrigerator and use them first.

Pressure Canning

This method is necessary for low-acid foods like vegetables, meat, poultry, and seafood, which are not safe to can using the water bath method due to the risk of botulism.

Materials:
   - Pressure canner
   - Canning jars, lids, and bands
   - Jar lifter and canning funnel
   - Ladle

Steps:

1. Prepare Jars:
   - Follow the same steps as in water bath canning to prepare jars and food.

2. Fill Jars and Apply Lids:
   - Follow the same steps as in water bath canning.

3. Process the Jars:
   - Place jars in the pressure canner with 2 to 3 inches of water.
   - Lock the canner lid and bring to a boil over medium-high heat.
   - Vent steam for 10 minutes, then close the vent.
   - Process according to the pressure and time dictated by your recipe, adjusting for altitude.

4. Allow Canner to Cool and Depressurize:
   - Once the processing time is complete, turn off the heat and let the canner cool and depressurize naturally.
   - Wait 10 to 15 minutes before opening the lid.

5. Remove Jars and Cool:
   - Remove jars, cool, and check seals exactly as in water bath canning.

Canning meat is a useful method to preserve it for long-term storage without the need for refrigeration. Here's how you can safely can meat at home using the pressure canning method, as this is the only safe method recommended for canning meat due to its low acidity:

Equipment Needed:
   - Pressure canner
   - Canning jars (pint or quart), lids, and rings
   - Jar lifter
   - Funnel
   - Clean cloths or paper towels

Ingredients:
   - Meat (beef, pork, chicken, turkey, etc.)
   - Salt (optional, for flavor)

Instructions:

Prepare the Meat

   Trim off any excess fat and cut the meat into cubes or strips, depending on your preference.

   Pre-cook (Optional) You can pre-cook the meat by roasting, stewing, or browning in a skillet. This step is optional but can enhance flavor and reduce some of the fats that could interfere with sealing.

Prepare the Jars

   Sterilize Jars: Although sterilizing jars is not necessary if you will be processing for more than 10 minutes, it is good practice to start with clean, hot jars. Wash them in hot, soapy water and rinse well.

   Heat Jars: Keep jars hot until ready to use to prevent them from breaking when filled with hot meat and liquid. You can keep them warm in a pot of simmering water or a heated dishwasher.

Pack the Meat

> Raw Pack: Fill jars with raw meat pieces, leaving 1-inch headspace at the top. Do not add liquid; the meat will produce its own juice.

> Hot Pack: If you pre-cooked the meat, pack it into the jars while hot, leaving 1-inch headspace. Pour in hot broth, water, or tomato juice (boiled for 5 minutes prior), still maintaining the 1-inch headspace.

Add Salt (Optional)

- You can add ½ teaspoon of salt per pint or 1 teaspoon per quart for flavor, but this is optional.

Remove Air Bubbles and Wipe Rims

- Run a non-metallic spatula or a bubble remover tool around the inside of the jar to remove air bubbles.
- Wipe the rim of each jar with a clean, damp cloth to remove any food particles or grease.

Seal the Jars

- Place the lids on the jars and screw on the rings until fingertip tight.

Process in a Pressure Canner

- Place the jars in the pressure canner. Follow the manufacturer's instructions for the amount of water to use.
- Lock the canner lid and bring it to a boil. Vent steam for 10 minutes, then close the vent.
- Process at 10 pounds of pressure (11 pounds for a dial gauge canner) for pints and 90 minutes for quarts. Adjust the pressure according to your altitude.

Cool Down

- After the processing time is complete, turn off the heat and let the pressure canner cool naturally. Do not open the vent or remove the weight until the pressure is fully released.
- Once depressurized, remove the lid and let the jars cool for 10 more minutes inside the canner.

Remove and Store Jars

- Use a jar lifter to carefully remove the jars from the canner and place them on a towel or cooling rack.
- Let jars cool for 24 hours. Check seals, then label and store in a cool, dark place.

Canning meat requires careful attention to processing times and pressures to ensure safety. Always refer to a reliable source like the USDA guidelines or the National Center for Home Food Preservation for specific instructions on canning different types of meat.

Canning fruit and vegetables is a great way to preserve your harvest and enjoy fresh produce year-round. The process involves placing prepared produce in jars and heating them to a temperature that destroys harmful microorganisms and creates a vacuum seal. Here's a step-by-step guide on how to can using the pressure canning method, which is necessary for low-acid vegetables:

Steps:

1. Prepare the Vegetables
   - -Thoroughly Wash and Peel
   - -Chop or Slice: Cut vegetables into uniform pieces to ensure even cooking and packing.

2. Prepare the Jars
   - -Sterilize Jars: Wash jars, lids, and bands in hot soapy water and rinse well. Keep jars warm in a pot of simmering water until ready to use to prevent them from breaking when filled with hot vegetables.
   - -Check Lids and Bands: Make sure lids and bands are free of rust and dents.

3. Blanch the Vegetables (Optional):
   - Blanching helps preserve the color, flavor, and nutritional value of vegetables. To blanch, place vegetables in boiling water for a few minutes, then immediately transfer them to an ice bath to stop the cooking process.

4. Pack the Jars:
   - Hot Pack: Boil the vegetables for a few minutes, then pack them into hot jars and cover with boiling water or broth, leaving 1 inch of headspace.
   - Raw Pack: Pack raw vegetables tightly into hot jars and cover with boiling water or broth, leaving 1 inch of headspace.

5. Remove Air Bubbles:
   - Use a non-metallic spatula or a bubble remover tool to remove air bubbles by sliding it around the inside edge of the jar. Add more liquid if necessary to maintain the proper headspace.

6. Wipe the Rims and Apply Lids:
   - Wipe the rims of the jars with a clean, damp cloth to ensure a good seal. Place the lids on the jars and screw the bands on until fingertip tight.

7. Load the Pressure Canner:
   - Follow the manufacturer's instructions for your pressure canner. Place a rack in the bottom of the canner and add the recommended amount of water. Load the jars onto the rack, ensuring they do not touch each other.

8. Process the Jars:
   - Secure the lid on the pressure canner and heat on high until steam flows steadily from the vent. Vent steam for 10 minutes, then close the vent or place the weight on the vent pipe.
   - Process the jars at the pressure recommended for your altitude (usually 10-15 pounds of pressure) for the specified time for the type of vegetable you are canning. Refer to reliable canning guides or the USDA for exact times and pressures.

9. Cool and Store the Jars:
   - Turn off the heat and allow the pressure to return to zero naturally. Wait 10 minutes before opening the canner. Carefully remove the jars using a jar lifter and place them on a towel or cooling rack.
   - Allow the jars to cool undisturbed for 12-24 hours. Check the seals by pressing down on the center of each lid. If it does not pop back, the jar is sealed. If any jars did not seal, refrigerate and use them within a few days.
   - Label the jars with the date and contents. Store in a cool, dark place. Properly canned vegetables can last for up to a year or more.

Safety Tips:
   - Use a Pressure Canner: Low-acid vegetables must be processed in a pressure canner to prevent the risk of botulism.
   - Follow Reliable Sources: Use canning guidelines from trusted sources such as the USDA or the National Center for Home Food Preservation.
   - Inspect Jars: Regularly check jars for signs of spoilage such as bulging lids, leaks, or off smells before consuming.

Here's a list of some of the easiest vegetables and fruits to can, ideal for beginners:

1. Tomatoes
   - Method: Water bath canning (with added acid like lemon juice or vinegar) or pressure canning. High acidity makes them versatile and easy to preserve.

2. Green Beans
   - Method: Pressure canning. Simple preparation and reliable results.

3. Carrots
   - Method: Pressure canning. Easy to peel and chop, and they maintain their texture well.

4. Peas
   - Method: Pressure canning. Quick to prepare and can well without losing flavor.

5. Corn
   - Method: Pressure canning. Straightforward shucking and cutting, retaining flavor and texture.

6. Peppers
   - Method: Water bath canning (pickled) or pressure canning. Can be canned whole, sliced, or diced, and great for adding to recipes.

7. Beets
   - Method: Pressure canning. Simple preparation and retain their flavor and color well.

8. Pumpkin
   - Method: Pressure canning (cubed). Easy to prepare, and versatile in recipes once canned.

9. Apples
   - Method: Water bath canning. Simple to peel, core, and slice; great for applesauce, pie filling, or slices.

10. Peaches
    - Method: Water bath canning. Easy to peel and slice, holding up well during canning.

11. Pears
    - Method: Water bath canning. Simple to peel and core, maintaining texture and flavor.

12. Berries (strawberries, blueberries, raspberries)
    - Method: Water bath canning. Minimal preparation needed, ideal for jams, jellies, or whole fruit canning.

13. Cherries
    - Method: Water bath canning. Easy to pit and can whole or as pie filling.

14. Plums
    - Method: Water bath canning. Require minimal preparation and maintain their shape and flavor.

15. Grapes
    - Method: Water bath canning. Can be canned whole.

16. Apricots
    - Method: Water bath canning. Simple to halve and pit, and great for preserves or canned halves.

17. Asparagus
    - Method: Pressure canning. Simple to prepare and holds its flavor and texture well.

18. Potatoes
    - Method: Pressure canning. Peeling and cubing potatoes are straightforward, and they are versatile in recipes.

19. Squash (Zucchini, Yellow Squash)
    - Method: Pressure canning (cubed). Easy to chop and can be used in soups and stews.

20. Spinach and Other Leafy Greens
    - Method: Pressure canning. Simple blanching process and retains nutritional value.

21. Cabbage (as sauerkraut)
    - Method: Water bath canning (fermented first). Fermentation is easy, and the final product cans well.

22. Mushrooms
    - Method: Pressure canning. Easy to clean and slice and maintain their flavor.

23. Mangoes
    - Method: Water bath canning. Simple to peel and slice, and great for canning in syrup.

24.. Pineapples
    - Method: Water bath canning. Easy to core and slice and hold up well in syrup.

25. Rhubarb
    - Method: Water bath canning. Minimal preparation, perfect for canning in syrups or as pie filling.

26. Figs
    - Method: Water bath canning. Easy to prepare and can be preserved whole or as jams.

27. Nectarines
    - Method: Water bath canning. No peeling required, just pit and slice.

28. Crabapples
    - Method: Water bath canning. Great for making crabapple jelly, easy to can whole.

General Tips for Easy Canning:
    - Follow Reliable Recipes: Use canning recipes from trusted sources like the USDA, Ball Canning, or the National Center for Home Food Preservation.
    - Sterilize Jars Properly: Ensure jars, lids, and bands are properly sterilized to prevent contamination.
    - Adjust for Altitude: Follow guidelines for adjusting processing times based on your altitude.
    - Label Jars: Always label your jars with the date and contents for easy identification and rotation.

- Use Fresh, High-Quality Produce: The quality of the produce you start with greatly impacts the final product. Use ripe, unblemished fruits and vegetables.
- Proper Headspace: Leave the recommended amount of headspace in jars to ensure proper sealing and to prevent overflow.
- Remove Air Bubbles: Use a non-metallic spatula or bubble remover tool to remove air bubbles before sealing jars.
- Wipe Jar Rims: Clean rims of jars with a damp cloth before placing lids to ensure a good seal.
- Store in a Cool, Dark Place: After canning, store your jars in a cool, dark place to maximize shelf life and maintain quality.

WHY IS KNOWING THE FERMENTATION PROCESS OF FRUITS AND VEGETABLES IMPORTANT?

Fermenting fruits and vegetables is a practice that offers a multitude of benefits, from extending shelf life to boosting health and enhancing culinary experiences. One of the primary reasons people turn to fermentation is for preservation. By creating an acidic environment, fermentation naturally inhibits the growth of harmful bacteria and mold, significantly extending the shelf life of fresh produce. This process is particularly valuable when dealing with seasonal abundance, allowing you to preserve fruits and vegetables at their peak and enjoy them throughout the year.

The health benefits of fermentation are another compelling reason to embrace this age-old technique. Fermented foods are rich in probiotics—beneficial bacteria that support gut health, improve digestion, and strengthen the immune system. The fermentation process also increases the bioavailability of nutrients, making vitamins and minerals more accessible to the body. Additionally, fermentation can detoxify certain foods, reducing toxins and making them safer and healthier to consume.

Fermentation also stands out as a sustainable and cost-effective practice. It helps reduce food waste by allowing you to ferment surplus or overripe produce that might otherwise be discarded. This not only makes efficient use of available resources but also provides a way to preserve food without relying on modern technology or refrigeration. Home fermentation can also save you money, as it reduces the need to buy commercially prepared fermented products.

Beyond preservation and sustainability, fermentation may contribute to potential health improvements. For those dealing with digestive issues like bloating, constipation, or irritable bowel syndrome (IBS), fermented foods can offer relief. There is also emerging research suggesting a connection between gut health and mental health, indicating that the probiotics found in fermented foods may positively impact mood and cognitive function.

Overall, fermenting fruits and vegetables is more than just a method of preservation—it's a practice that enhances the flavor, health, and sustainability of your diet. Whether you're interested in the health benefits, the taste, or the tradition, fermentation is a time-tested technique that continues to offer valuable advantages in our modern world.

Fermenting fruits and vegetables is a traditional preservation method that relies on natural processes and doesn't require electricity. Here's a step-by-step guide on how to ferment fruits and vegetables:

Materials:
- Fresh fruits and vegetables
- Sharp knife
- Cutting board
- Sea salt or kosher salt (non-iodized)
- Water (non-chlorinated)
- Fermentation vessels (glass jars, ceramic crocks, or food-grade plastic containers)
- Weights (to keep the produce submerged)
- Cheesecloth or breathable fabric
- Rubber bands or string

Steps:

1. Prepare the Fruits and Vegetables:
   - Select the Produce: Choose fresh, high-quality fruits and vegetables. Wash them thoroughly to remove dirt and contaminants.
   - Cut and Prepare: Chop, slice, or shred the fruits and vegetables as desired. Uniform sizes help ensure even fermentation.

2. Create a Brine:
   - Salt Brine: Dissolve 1-3 tablespoons of sea salt or kosher salt in 1 quart (1 liter) of water. The exact amount of salt will depend on the type of produce and your taste preferences.
   - For Sauerkraut: Use about 1 tablespoon of salt per 1.5 pounds (0.7 kg) of cabbage.
   - For Cucumbers: Use 2-3 tablespoons of salt per quart (1 liter) of water.

3. Pack the Fermentation Vessels:
   - Layer and Pack: Place the prepared fruits or vegetables into the fermentation vessels. Pack them tightly to minimize air pockets.
   - Add Brine: Pour the brine over the packed produce, ensuring that it is completely submerged. Leave some headspace at the top of the vessel to allow for expansion during fermentation.

4. Weigh Down the Produce:
   - Use Weights: Place weights on top of the produce to keep it submerged under the brine. This can be a fermentation weight, a small plate with a clean rock, or a zip-top bag filled with brine.

5. Cover and Store:
   - Cover: Cover the fermentation vessel with cheesecloth or breathable fabric to keep out dust and insects while allowing gases to escape. Secure the cover with a rubber band or string.
   - Store: Store the vessel in a cool, dark place, such as a pantry or basement, where the temperature is consistently between 60-75°F (16-24°C).

6. Monitor the Fermentation:
   - Check Daily: Check the fermentation daily to ensure the produce remains submerged and to remove any mold or scum that forms on the surface.

- Taste Test: Start tasting the fermented produce after a few days. Fermentation times will vary depending on the temperature, type of produce, and desired tanginess. Most vegetables will ferment in 1-4 weeks, while fruits may ferment more quickly.

7. Finish and Store:
   - Stop Fermentation: Once the desired flavor and texture are achieved, remove the weights and cover the vessel with a lid.
   - Refrigerate: Transfer the fermented produce to the refrigerator or a cool storage area to slow down the fermentation process and preserve the flavor. Fermented fruits and vegetables can last for several months when stored properly.

Tips:

- Clean Equipment: Ensure all equipment and vessels are clean to avoid contamination.
- Non-Chlorinated Water: Use non-chlorinated water to avoid inhibiting the fermentation process.
- Consistent Temperature: Maintain a consistent temperature to ensure proper fermentation.
- Label and Date: Label and date your fermentation vessels for easy tracking.

Doomsday Booze

Being in a doomsday situation will be rough, and who wouldn't want to wind down in front of the fire pit after a long, stressful day with a glass of your favorite drink to warm your belly? Making alcohol from fermented fruit, commonly known as fruit wine, involves fermenting the natural sugars in the fruit with yeast. Here is a step-by-step guide to making alcohol from fermented fruit:

Materials:
- Fresh fruit (apples, grapes, berries, peaches, etc.)
- Sugar (optional, depending on the fruit's natural sugar content)
- Water (non-chlorinated)
- Wine yeast (available at brewing supply stores)
- Fermentation vessel (glass carboy, food-grade plastic bucket, or ceramic crock)
- Airlock (to release gases while keeping air out)
- Clean cloth or cheesecloth
- Sanitizer (for cleaning equipment)
- Siphoning tube
- Bottles with airtight seals

Steps:
1. Prepare the Fruit:
   - Select the Fruit: Choose ripe, high-quality fruit. Wash it thoroughly to remove dirt and contaminants.
   - Chop and Crush: Remove any stems, pits, or seeds, then chop the fruit into small pieces. Crush the fruit to release the juices. This can be done with a potato masher or by hand.

2. Make the Must:
   - Create the Must: Place the crushed fruit into the fermentation vessel. If needed, add sugar to increase the alcohol content (about 1-2 pounds of sugar per gallon of must, depending on the fruit's natural sugar content).
   - Add Water: Add enough water to cover the fruit and reach the desired volume (usually about 1 gallon for home batches).

3. Add the Yeast:
   - Prepare the Yeast: Follow the instructions on the yeast package to rehydrate it (if necessary).
   - Add Yeast: Sprinkle the yeast over the must and stir it in. Wine yeast is preferred over bread yeast as it produces better flavors and higher alcohol content.

4. Primary Fermentation:
   - Cover and Ferment: Cover the vessel with a clean cloth or cheesecloth and secure it with a rubber band. This allows gases to escape while keeping out contaminants.
   - Stir Daily: Stir the must daily with a sanitized spoon to mix the fruit and release gases.
   - Monitor Fermentation: Fermentation should start within 24-48 hours, indicated by bubbles and a frothy surface. This primary fermentation lasts about 5-7 days.

5. Secondary Fermentation:
  - Strain the Must: After primary fermentation, strain the liquid to remove the solid fruit pieces. Pour the liquid into a clean fermentation vessel.
  - Attach Airlock: Fit the vessel with an airlock to allow gases to escape while preventing air from entering.
  - Ferment Further: Allow the liquid to ferment for several weeks to several months. The fermentation speed will depend on the temperature and the specific fruit used.

6. Clarification:
  - Racking: Once fermentation is complete (when bubbles stop forming), siphon the liquid into a clean container, leaving behind the sediment (lees). This process, known as racking, can be done several times over the course of a few months to clarify the wine.

7. Bottling:
  - Sanitize Bottles: Thoroughly sanitize the bottles and caps or corks.
  - Bottle the Wine: Siphon the clarified wine into the bottles, leaving a little headspace. Seal the bottles with airtight caps or corks.

8. Aging:
  - Age the Wine: Store the bottles in a cool, dark place for several months to a year to allow the flavors to mature and improve.

9. Enjoy:
  - Taste: After aging, the wine is ready to drink. Enjoy your homemade fruit wine responsibly.

Tips:
  - Clean Equipment: Ensure all equipment is sanitized to prevent contamination.
  - Monitor Temperature: Maintain a consistent fermentation temperature (typically 60-75°F or 16-24°C).
  - Patience: The longer the wine ages, the better it will taste. Be patient and allow sufficient time for fermentation and aging.

By following these steps, you can make your own alcohol from fermented fruit, creating a unique and flavorful homemade fruit wine.

Butter

Canning butter at home is not recommended by the USDA or other food safety authorities due to safety concerns. Butter is a low-acid food, which means that if it is not processed correctly, it poses a risk of botulism—a serious form of food poisoning. Home canning equipment cannot reliably reach the high temperatures needed to safely process low-acid foods like butter.

However, for those who are looking for long-term storage solutions for butter, there are alternative preservation methods that are considered safer:

Freezing

Butter can be frozen in its original packaging or wrapped tightly in aluminum foil or plastic wrap to prevent freezer burn. Properly stored, butter can last in the freezer for up to a year.

Butter Powder

Commercial butter powder is another alternative. This is butter that has been dehydrated and can be stored for a long duration.

- Usage: It can be used in baking or reconstituted with water to make spreadable butter.
- Storage: Keep it in a cool, dry place, and it can last for several years.

If you still wish to preserve butter at home in a way that involves canning, it's crucial to follow safe practices and possibly consult with a food preservation expert. Always prioritize safety and consider reliable preservation methods approved by food safety authorities.

Ghee

For a butter alternative, consider making and storing ghee in your everyday life as well preparing for hard times, and here's why:

1. High Smoke Point:
   - Ghee has a high smoke point (around 485°F or 252°C), making it ideal for frying and sautéing without breaking down and releasing harmful compounds.

2. Enhanced Flavor:
   - Ghee has a rich, nutty flavor that can enhance the taste of various dishes, providing a more intense and complex taste than regular butter.

3. Long Shelf Life:
   - Ghee is shelf-stable and does not require refrigeration. It can be stored at room temperature for several months without spoiling, as the removal of milk solids eliminates moisture.

4. It can replace butter, oil, or other fats in most recipes.

5. Lactose and Casein-Free:
   - The process of making ghee removes milk solids, making it suitable for individuals who are lactose intolerant or have casein sensitivities.

6. Rich in Healthy Fats:
   - Ghee contains beneficial fats, including short-chain and medium-chain fatty acids, which are easier to digest and can provide a quick source of energy.

7. Source of Fat-Soluble Vitamins:
   - Ghee is a good source of fat-soluble vitamins such as A, D, E, and K. These vitamins are essential for various bodily functions, including immune support, bone health, and skin health.

8. Anti-Inflammatory Properties:
   - Ghee contains butyrate, a short-chain fatty acid that has been shown to have anti-inflammatory properties and can support gut health.

9. Contains CLA:
   - Ghee contains conjugated linoleic acid (CLA), which has been associated with various health benefits, including reduced body fat and improved metabolic health.

Ghee is easy to make at home with minimal equipment and ingredients, allowing for control over the quality and purity of the final product. Making ghee yourself is also more cost-effective than buying commercially produced ghee, especially if you purchase butter in bulk. Simply cook butter to separate the milk solids and water from the butterfat. Here's a step-by-step guide to making ghee:

Ingredients:
   - Unsalted butter (as much as you want to convert into ghee)

Equipment:
- Medium to large saucepan
- Spoon or spatula
- Fine mesh strainer or cheesecloth
- Clean, dry jar for storage

Instructions:

1. Melt the Butter:
- Place the butter in a medium saucepan. Use a heavy-bottomed pan if possible to prevent burning.
- Melt the butter over medium heat. Allow it to come to a simmer.

2. Simmer and Separate:
- Once the butter starts simmering, reduce the heat to low. You'll notice foam forming on the top and milk solids beginning to separate and sink to the bottom.
- Let the butter simmer gently. The butter will go through several stages of foaming and bubbling. This is the moisture evaporating and the milk solids cooking.

3. Watch the Color and Clarity:
- As it cooks, the butter will become clearer, and the milk solids at the bottom of the pan will turn golden brown. The bubbling will decrease significantly, and you might hear a crackling sound. This process can take anywhere from 15 to 30 minutes depending on the amount of butter used.

4. Check for Doneness:
- The ghee is done when the butter is golden and translucent, and the solids at the bottom are caramel brown, not burnt. The characteristic nutty aroma of ghee will be apparent.

5. Strain the Ghee:
- Remove the pan from heat and let the ghee cool for a few minutes. Then strain it through a fine mesh strainer lined with cheesecloth into a clean, dry jar. The cheesecloth will catch all the milk solids, leaving you with clear ghee.

6. Store the Ghee:
- Allow the ghee to cool completely before sealing the jar. Ghee can be stored at room temperature or in the refrigerator. At room temperature, ghee can last up to a month, and when refrigerated, it can last up to a year.

Tips:
- Quality of Butter: The quality of your ghee greatly depends on the quality of the butter. Grass-fed butter is often recommended for its flavor and nutritional content.
- Monitoring: Keep a close eye on the ghee as it simmers, especially towards the end, to prevent the solids from burning.
- Storage: Store ghee in airtight containers to keep out moisture and other contaminants.

Ghee is a versatile ingredient in cooking, suitable for high-heat cooking due to its high smoke point, and it adds a rich, nutty flavor to dishes. Enjoy using your homemade ghee in various culinary preparations.

THE IMPORTANCE OF TALLOW

Tallow has been a staple in traditional medicine for centuries, valued for its healing properties and easy availability as a natural byproduct of animal husbandry. Across various cultures, this nutrient-rich fat has been utilized in numerous ways, making it a versatile remedy in folk healing practices.

One of the primary uses of tallow in traditional medicine is skincare and healing. Tallow is a powerful moisturizer packed with vitamins A, D, E, K, and B12 and essential minerals. It has been applied to dry, chapped skin and treats cuts, burns, and abrasions, promoting faster healing and protecting the skin. Beyond its benefits for the skin, tallow also soothes joint and muscle pain. In the form of balms and rubs, massage into sore muscles and stiff joints, with its fatty acids believed to reduce inflammation and discomfort.

In some cultures, tallow has played a role in respiratory health. Mixed with herbs, it was traditionally used as a chest rub to alleviate symptoms of colds, flu, and bronchitis, helping to clear congestion and ease breathing. Additionally, tallow serves as an effective carrier for other remedial ingredients. Combined with medicinal herbs and essential oils, it forms salves and ointments that deliver therapeutic properties deep into the skin, enhancing their effectiveness.

Tallow's uses extend even further. Historically, it has been applied as a wound dressing, creating a protective barrier that keeps wounds moist and promotes faster healing by preventing hard scabs from forming. Its soothing properties have also made it a go-to remedy for treating rashes, eczema, and other skin irritations, helping to reduce itching and inflammation while aiding in skin repair.

Tallow-based products can also boost the immune system, with the fat-soluble vitamins and beneficial fatty acids believed to nourish the body and support overall health. While modern medical science often calls for more empirical evidence to fully endorse these traditional uses, the enduring presence of tallow in natural health practices speaks to its perceived effectiveness and natural origin.

Today, even as science advances, many people turn to tallow for its time-honored healing qualities, keeping this ancient remedy alive in the realm of natural health and wellness. Its rich history and multifaceted applications make it a fascinating example of how traditional knowledge continues to influence modern approaches to health.

Tallow, rendered from the fat of cows or sheep, is a versatile substance with a wide range of uses across various fields. Here are 20 ways in which tallow can be used:

1. Cooking: High smoke point makes it excellent for frying, sautéing, and grilling.

2. Baking: Used as a substitute for butter or shortening in recipes like pies and pastries.

3. Candle Making: Tallow candles are a traditional source of light and can burn brightly and for long durations.

4. Soap Making: Provides a hard, long-lasting soap with creamy lather.

5. Skincare: Used in creams and lotions as it is naturally moisturizing and similar in composition to human skin oils.

6. Lip Balm: Acts as a base for homemade lip balms to nourish and protect lips.

7. Conditioning Leather: Tallow can be used to condition and waterproof leather goods like boots and jackets.

8. Waterproofing Canvas: Used to waterproof canvas items such as tents and tarps.

9. Rust Protection: Coating metal tools and surfaces to prevent rust.

10. Lubrication: Useful in lubricating machinery where petroleum products are unsuitable.

11. Bird Food: Mixed with birdseed to make suet cakes for feeding birds during the winter.

12. Traditional Medicine: Used in various traditional medicinal preparations for its supposed healing properties.

13. Hair Care: Incorporated into conditioners and balms to nourish and strengthen hair.

14. Pet Food: Added to pet food to improve coat health and provide energy.

15. Hand Cream: Used as a barrier cream to protect and heal dry and cracked hands.

16. Deer Bait: Used as a lure for hunting deer since it is high in fat and attractive to them.

17. Shaving Cream: Makes a dense and slippery shaving cream.

18. Fishing Bait: Some fishermen use tallow as bait or additive in bait for certain types of fish.

19. Wood Treatment: Used for treating and finishing wood products.

20. Cast Iron Seasoning: Effective for seasoning cast iron cookware to create a non-stick surface.

Tallow's rich consistency and high fat content make it incredibly useful for these diverse applications, making it a valuable resource in households and various industries.

Making tallow involves rendering beef or mutton fat into a clear, pure fat that solidifies at room temperature. Tallow is highly valued for its use in cooking, soap making, and as a natural moisturizer. Here's how to make tallow at home:

Ingredients:
- Beef fat (suet) or mutton fat

Equipment:
- Large pot or slow cooker
- Strainer
- Cheesecloth or fine mesh sieve
- Containers for storing tallow

Instructions:

1. Prepare the Fat:
   - Start by obtaining fat from beef or mutton, preferably from around the kidneys and loins, which is known as suet. This fat is the cleanest and has the least connective tissue.
   - Trim off any meat or blood vessels from the fat. This is important as impurities can affect the flavor and shelf life of the tallow.
   - Chop the fat into small pieces, or for better and quicker rendering, grind the fat using a meat grinder or food processor.

2. Start the Rendering Process:
   - Place the chopped or ground fat into a large pot or a slow cooker. Set the heat to low. You want to melt the fat slowly to prevent burning and ensure even rendering.
   - As the fat slowly heats, it will begin to melt, and liquid fat will accumulate while the solid impurities will settle.

3. Stir Occasionally:
   - Stir the fat occasionally to ensure that it melts evenly and doesn't stick to the bottom of the pot.
   - In a slow cooker, this process can take several hours, depending on the amount of fat. If using a stovetop, expect it to take a few hours as well.

4. Strain the Fat:
   - Once the fat has mostly melted and you see crispy bits settled at the bottom, which are the impurities and connective tissues, it's time to strain.
   - Set a strainer over a large bowl or pot and line it with cheesecloth or a fine mesh sieve. Carefully pour the hot fat through the strainer to remove all the solids.

5. Store the Tallow:
   - Pour the strained liquid tallow into containers for storage. Glass jars are ideal as they can handle the hot fat without risk of melting.
   - Allow the tallow to cool at room temperature. As it cools, it will solidify and turn white.
   - Seal the containers and store the tallow in a cool, dark place or refrigerate it. Properly rendered and stored tallow can last for months or even years without spoiling.

Tips:

-   Low and Slow: The key to rendering tallow is to keep the heat low to prevent burning the fat.
-   Usage: Tallow can be used for frying, sautéing, or as a dairy-free alternative to butter. It's also great for making candles, soaps, and skin care products due to its moisturizing properties.

Rendering tallow is a straightforward process that offers a range of uses in the kitchen and beyond. Enjoy exploring the many benefits and uses of your homemade tallow.

DEHYDRATING FRUITS, VEGETABLES, AND MEATS IN A DOOMSDAY SITUATION

Being prepared before disaster hits is important, but what happens when the electricity goes out and doesn't come back on? How do you plan to keep your stores full of food that will last?

Dehydrating fruit in a hot car can be an effective method if done carefully, as the car can act like a solar dehydrator. Here's a step-by-step guide to safely dehydrate fruit in a hot car:

Materials:
- Fresh fruit
- Sharp knife
- Cutting board
- Lemon juice or ascorbic acid solution (optional, to prevent browning)
- Baking sheets or trays
- Parchment paper or silicone baking mats
- Cheesecloth or fine mesh (to protect from insects and debris)
- Car with windows that can be slightly opened

Steps:

1. Prepare the Fruits:
   - Select the Fruits: Choose ripe, high-quality fruits. Wash them thoroughly to remove dirt and contaminants.
   - Cut and Prepare: Peel, core, and slice the fruit into uniform pieces. Thin slices (1/4 inch or less) dry faster and more evenly. Remove any pits or seeds.

2. Prevent Browning (Optional):
   - Dip in Solution: To prevent browning of light-colored fruits like apples, pears, and bananas, dip the fruit slices in a solution of lemon juice and water (1:1 ratio) or ascorbic acid solution for a few minutes. Drain well and pat dry.

3. Set Up for Dehydrating in the Car:
   - Prepare the Trays: Line baking sheets or trays with parchment paper or silicone baking mats to prevent sticking. Place the fruit slices in a single layer on the trays, ensuring they do not overlap.
   - Cover the Fruit: Place cheesecloth or fine mesh over the fruit slices to protect them from insects and debris.

4. Place the Trays in the Car:
   - Choose the Right Time: Start in the morning on a hot, sunny day to take advantage of the maximum heat.
   - Position the Trays: Place the trays on the dashboard, rear window shelf, or seats where they will receive the most sunlight. Ensure they are stable and won't tip over.
   - Ventilate the Car: Slightly open the windows to allow moisture to escape and to maintain airflow. Be careful not to open them too much, as you want to keep the interior hot.

5. Monitor the Drying Process:
   - Check Regularly: Check the fruit every few hours to monitor progress and ensure it is drying evenly. Rotate the trays if necessary.
   - Temperature and Time: The temperature inside the car can reach 120-150°F (49-65°C) or higher on a hot day. Drying time will vary depending on the fruit and thickness of the slices, typically taking 1-2 days.

6. Check for Doneness:
   - Test for Dryness: The fruit is done when it is leathery and pliable but not sticky or moist. There should be no visible moisture when the fruit is torn apart.

7. Condition and Store:
   - Conditioning: Place the dried fruit in a loosely packed container for a week, shaking it daily to distribute any remaining moisture evenly. This step helps prevent mold.
   - Store Properly: Store the conditioned dried fruit in airtight containers or vacuum-sealed bags. Keep the containers in a cool, dark place or refrigerate/freeze them for longer shelf life.

Tips:
   - Safety First: Do not leave pets or children in the car while dehydrating fruit.
   - Uniform Slices: Cutting the fruit into uniform slices ensures even drying.
   - Weather Conditions: Choose a day with low humidity to speed up the drying process and reduce the risk of mold.

Building food dehydrators that don't need electricity can be a rewarding project and allows you to preserve food using solar energy or natural airflow. Here are two methods: a solar dehydrator and a simple air-drying dehydrator.

Building a Solar Dehydrator

Materials:

- Plywood or wooden boards
- Glass or clear plastic sheets
- Wire mesh or food-safe screens
- Hinges
- Nails or screws
- Black paint (optional, for better heat absorption)
- Ventilation holes or adjustable vents
- Saw, hammer, screwdriver, drill

Steps:

1. Design the Frame:

- Decide the size of your dehydrator based on how much food you plan to dry. A common size is about 3 feet high, 2 feet wide, and 1.5 feet deep.
- Build the frame using plywood or wooden boards. Construct a slanted roof to maximize sun exposure.

2. Construct the Drying Chamber:

- Install wire mesh or food-safe screens as shelves inside the frame. These should be spaced about 4-6 inches apart to allow airflow.
- Ensure the shelves are removable or adjustable for versatility.

3. Install the Solar Collector:

- Paint the interior of the dehydrator black to absorb more heat (optional but recommended).
- Attach glass or clear plastic sheets to the front or top of the dehydrator to act as a solar collector. The slanted roof should also be covered with the clear material.
- Ensure the collector is securely attached and sealed to retain heat.

4. Ventilation:

- Drill ventilation holes near the top and bottom of the dehydrator. These allow hot air to rise and exit while drawing in cooler air from below.
- Install adjustable vents if you want more control over airflow.

5. Hinged Door:

- Attach a hinged door to the front of the dehydrator for easy access to the drying trays.
- Ensure the door has a good seal to retain heat.

6. Positioning:

- Place the dehydrator in a sunny location, ideally facing south (in the Northern Hemisphere) to maximize sun exposure.
- Elevate the dehydrator on blocks or legs to improve airflow.

Solar Dehydrator

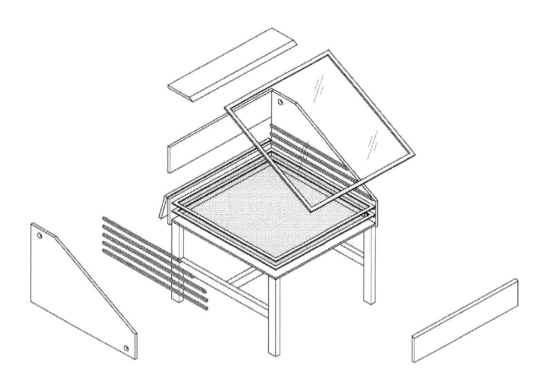

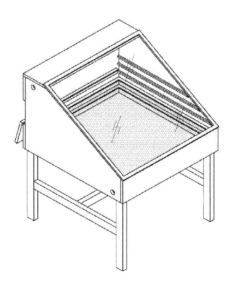

Building an Air-Drying Dehydrator

Materials:
- -Wooden frame or repurposed wooden box
- Wire mesh or food-safe screens
- Cheesecloth or fine mesh (to protect from insects)
- Nails or screws
- Saw, hammer, screwdriver

Steps:

1. Design the Frame:
   - Build or repurpose a wooden frame or box. Ensure it is sturdy and has enough space for multiple shelves.

2. Construct Shelves:
   - Install wire mesh or food-safe screens as shelves inside the frame. These should be spaced about 4-6 inches apart.
   - Ensure the shelves are removable or adjustable.

3. Ventilation:
   - Drill several ventilation holes on the sides of the frame. Proper ventilation is crucial for effective air drying.
   - Cover the ventilation holes with cheesecloth or fine mesh to keep insects out.

   - 4. Protect the Food:
   - Attach cheesecloth or fine mesh to the top of the frame to protect the food from insects and debris.

5. Positioning:
   - Place the dehydrator in a dry, well-ventilated area, preferably outdoors in a shaded spot to avoid direct sunlight, which can degrade some nutrients.
   - Elevate the dehydrator on blocks or legs to improve airflow.

Tips:
- Uniform Slices: Cut food into uniform slices to ensure even drying.
- Rotate Trays: Regularly rotate trays for even drying.
- Monitor Weather: For solar dehydrators, monitor weather conditions to ensure consistent drying.
- Check Regularly: Regularly check the food for dryness and remove any pieces that are done to avoid over-drying.

By following these steps, you can build an effective food dehydrator without electricity, utilizing natural methods to preserve your food.

Air-Drying Dehydrator

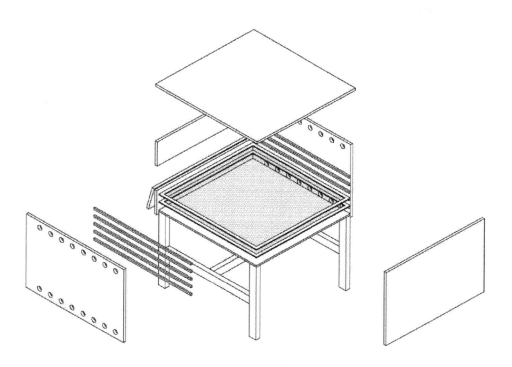

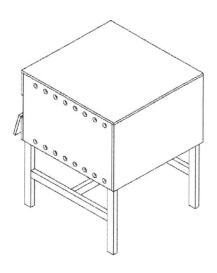

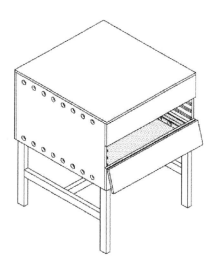

Dehydrating meat is a process that involves removing moisture to preserve the meat for longer periods. Here's a step-by-step guide on how to dehydrate meat:

Materials:

- Lean meat (beef, chicken, turkey, or game meat)
- Sharp knife
- Cutting board
- Marinade (optional)
- Dehydrator (or an oven with a low-temperature setting)
- Meat thermometer
- Airtight storage containers

Steps:

1. Select the Meat:

- Choose lean cuts of meat with minimal fat, as fat does not dehydrate well and can spoil.
- Popular choices include beef (round, flank, or sirloin), chicken breast, or turkey breast.

2. Prepare the Meat:

- Trim any visible fat from the meat.
- Slice the meat into thin, even strips, about 1/8 to 1/4 inch thick. Thinner slices will dehydrate more quickly and evenly.

3. Marinate the Meat (Optional):

- If you want to add flavor, marinate the meat strips in your preferred marinade for 4-24 hours in the refrigerator. Popular marinades include soy sauce, Worcestershire sauce, garlic, onion powder, and pepper.
- Pat the meat strips dry with paper towels after marinating.

4. Pre-Treat the Meat (Optional):

- To ensure safety and kill any bacteria, you can pre-treat the meat by steaming it for 10 minutes or boiling it briefly before dehydrating. Use a meat thermometer to ensure the internal temperature reaches at least 160°F (71°C) for beef or 165°F (74°C) for poultry.

5. Arrange the Meat in the Dehydrator:

- Place the meat strips in a single layer on the dehydrator trays, ensuring they do not overlap.
- If using an oven, place the meat on wire racks over baking sheets to allow air circulation.

6. Dehydrate the Meat:

- Set the dehydrator to 140°F (60°C) and dehydrate for 4-8 hours. The drying time will vary depending on the thickness of the slices and the type of meat.
- If using an oven, set it to the lowest possible temperature (usually around 140°F to 170°F). Prop the oven door open slightly to allow moisture to escape and maintain airflow. Dehydrate for 6-12 hours, checking periodically.

7. Check for Doneness:

- The meat is done when it is dry, leathery, and brittle but not crumbly. It should bend and crack but not snap.
- Test a piece by cutting it open; there should be no visible moisture inside.

8. Cool and Store:

- Allow the dehydrated meat to cool completely to room temperature.
- Store the dehydrated meat in airtight containers or vacuum-sealed bags. For long-term storage, keep the containers in a cool, dark place or refrigerate/freeze them.

Tips:

- Uniform Slices: Ensuring uniform thickness of meat slices helps in even drying.
- Moisture Check: Check for moisture after the first few hours and rotate trays if necessary for even drying.
- Safety First: Always use a meat thermometer to ensure the meat reaches a safe temperature during the pre-treatment and drying processes.

By following these steps, you can successfully dehydrate meat and enjoy your homemade jerky or dried meat for weeks or even months.

Dehydrating vegetables is a great way to preserve them for long-term storage while retaining most of their nutritional value. Here's a step-by-step guide on how to dehydrate vegetables:

Materials:

- Fresh vegetables
- Sharp knife
- Cutting board
- Large pot for blanching (optional)
- Ice water (optional)
- Dehydrator (or an oven with a low-temperature setting)
- Airtight storage containers or vacuum-sealed bags

Steps:

1. Select the Vegetables:

   - Choose fresh, high-quality vegetables. Wash them thoroughly to remove dirt and contaminants.

2. Prepare the Vegetables:

   - Cut the vegetables into uniform pieces. Smaller pieces will dehydrate more quickly and evenly. For example, slice carrots and zucchini into thin rounds, chop broccoli and cauliflower into small florets, and cut bell peppers into strips or small chunks.

3. Blanch the Vegetables (Optional but Recommended):

   - Blanching helps to preserve the color, flavor, and nutritional value of vegetables.
   - Bring a large pot of water to a boil. Prepare a bowl of ice water.
   - Place the vegetables in the boiling water for 2-5 minutes, depending on the vegetable (e.g., 3 minutes for carrots, 2 minutes for green beans).
   - Immediately transfer the blanched vegetables to the ice water to stop the cooking process. Drain well and pat dry.

4. Arrange the Vegetables in the Dehydrator:

   - Place the vegetable pieces in a single layer on the dehydrator trays, ensuring they do not overlap.
   - If using an oven, place the vegetables on wire racks over baking sheets to allow air circulation.

5. Dehydrate the Vegetables:

   - Set the dehydrator to 125°F to 135°F (52°C to 57°C) and dehydrate for 6-12 hours. The drying time will vary depending on the type and size of the vegetables.
   - If using an oven, set it to the lowest possible temperature (usually around 140°F to 170°F). Prop the oven door open slightly to allow moisture to escape and maintain airflow. Dehydrate for 6-12 hours, checking periodically.

6. Check for Doneness:

   - Vegetables are done when they are brittle and snap when bent. There should be no signs of moisture when the vegetables are broken apart.

7. Cool and Store:

   - Allow the dehydrated vegetables to cool completely to room temperature.

- Store the dehydrated vegetables in airtight containers or vacuum-sealed bags. For long-term storage, keep the containers in a cool, dark place or refrigerate/freeze them.

Tips:

- Uniform Pieces: Cutting vegetables into uniform sizes helps in even drying.
- Air Circulation: Ensure proper air circulation by not overcrowding the trays.
- Label and Date: Label and date your containers for easy identification and to keep track of storage time.
- Rehydration: To rehydrate, soak the dried vegetables in water or broth for 1-2 hours before using them in recipes.

By following these steps, you can successfully dehydrate vegetables and enjoy them for months, preserving their flavors and nutritional benefits.

Dehydrating fruit is an excellent way to preserve it for long-term storage while retaining its sweetness and nutrients. Here's a step-by-step guide on how to dehydrate fruit:

Materials:

- Fresh fruit
- Sharp knife
- Cutting board
- Large pot for blanching (optional)
- Lemon juice or ascorbic acid solution (optional)
- Dehydrator (or an oven with a low-temperature setting)
- Airtight storage containers or vacuum-sealed bags

Steps:

1. Select the Fruit:

   - Choose ripe, high-quality fruit. Wash it thoroughly to remove dirt and contaminants.

2. Prepare the Fruit:

   - Peel, core, and slice the fruit into uniform pieces. Smaller pieces will dehydrate more quickly and evenly. For example, slice apples and pears into thin rings or wedges, halve or slice strawberries, and cut bananas into thin rounds.

3. Prevent Browning (Optional):

   - To prevent browning of light-colored fruits like apples, pears, and bananas, dip the fruit slices in a solution of lemon juice and water (1:1 ratio) or ascorbic acid solution for a few minutes. Drain well and pat dry.

4. Blanch the Fruit (Optional):

   - Blanching is generally not necessary for most fruits, but it can help preserve the color and texture of some fruits like peaches and apricots.
   - Bring a large pot of water to a boil. Prepare a bowl of ice water.
   - Place the fruit in the boiling water for 1-2 minutes, then immediately transfer it to the ice water to stop the cooking process. Drain well and pat dry.

5. Arrange the Fruit in the Dehydrator:

   - Place the fruit pieces in a single layer on the dehydrator trays, ensuring they do not overlap.
   - If using an oven, place the fruit on wire racks over baking sheets to allow air circulation.

6. Dehydrate the Fruit:

   - Set the dehydrator to 135°F to 145°F (57°C to 63°C) and dehydrate for 6-12 hours. The drying time will vary depending on the type and size of the fruit.
   - If using an oven, set it to the lowest possible temperature (usually around 140°F to 170°F). Prop the oven door open slightly to allow moisture to escape and maintain airflow. Dehydrate for 6-12 hours, checking periodically.

7. Check for Doneness:

   - Fruit is done when it is leathery and pliable but not sticky or moist. It should not have any visible moisture when torn apart.

8. Cool and Store:
   - Allow the dehydrated fruit to cool completely to room temperature.
   - Store the dehydrated fruit in airtight containers or vacuum-sealed bags. For long-term storage, keep the containers in a cool, dark place or refrigerate/freeze them.

Tips:
   - Uniform Slices: Ensuring uniform thickness of fruit slices helps in even drying.
   - Air Circulation: Ensure proper air circulation by not overcrowding the trays.
   - Label and Date: Label and date your containers for easy identification and to keep track of storage time.
   - Rehydration: To rehydrate, soak the dried fruit in water or juice for a few hours before using them in recipes, or enjoy them as is for a tasty snack.

By following these steps, you can successfully dehydrate fruit and enjoy it for months, preserving its natural flavors and nutrients.

Build Your Own Smoker

Building an outdoor smoker can be a rewarding project, giving you the ability to smoke your own meats, fish, and vegetables right in your backyard. A smoker is designed to cook food at low temperatures for extended periods of time, allowing smoke to infuse rich, deep flavors into the food. Here's a step-by-step guide to building a simple, functional outdoor smoker.

Metal Smoker

Materials:

-   Metal drum (e.g., 55-gallon steel drum) or brick/stone for the main smoking chamber
-   Grates (stainless steel or cast iron) for cooking surfaces
-   Firebox or charcoal basket (steel or metal grating)
-   Heat-resistant paint (optional for a drum smoker)
-   Chimney or ventilation pipe
-   Metal sheets or stones/bricks (for airflow control)
-   Temperature gauge
-   Drill and hole saw (for metal)
-   Metal cutting tools (if using a metal drum)

Step 1: Choose Your Design

There are a few different designs you can choose for building a smoker:

1. Drum Smoker: Uses a large metal drum (like a 55-gallon barrel) as the main smoking chamber. It's an easier option for beginners.
2. Offset Smoker: This design includes two separate sections—one for the fire (the firebox) and one for the smoking chamber. Smoke and heat travel from the firebox into the chamber, providing indirect heat.
3. Brick or Stone Smoker: A more permanent and durable option, this smoker is made from bricks, cinder blocks, or stones and requires a bit more effort and skill but offers excellent insulation.

For simplicity, we'll focus on a drum smoker as it is a common DIY project that is effective and easier to build.

Step 2: Prepare the Drum

If you are using a 55-gallon steel drum, you need to ensure it's clean and safe for use with food. Avoid drums that have held chemicals or hazardous substances.

1. Clean the Drum: Burn out any residue inside the drum by lighting a fire inside and letting it burn for several hours to remove paint, oils, and any other materials. After cooling, scrub it out thoroughly with steel wool and soap to ensure it's clean.
2. Cut Openings:
    -   Drill several holes near the bottom of the drum to allow airflow to feed the fire. These should be about 1 to 2 inches in diameter and evenly spaced around the bottom.
    -   Cut a hole at the top or on the side of the drum for the chimney or exhaust vent. This helps control the smoke and temperature. Use a hole saw or metal cutting tool for this.

- Attach a metal pipe or chimney to this hole to allow the smoke to exit while still controlling airflow.

Step 3: Install Grates and Charcoal Basket

1. Charcoal Basket: At the bottom of the drum, install a charcoal basket or a small firebox. This can be made from expanded metal or steel grates fashioned into a basket that holds your charcoal or wood. Position it so there's enough space below for air to circulate and fuel the fire.
2. Cooking Grates: Install one or two metal grates above the charcoal basket for your food. These can be placed at different heights depending on the size of the drum. Drill holes into the sides of the drum and insert bolts or metal rods to hold the grates in place.

Step 4: Add Airflow Control

Controlling the airflow is crucial for maintaining a steady smoking temperature, usually between 225-250°F.

1. Air Intake: Install a sliding or rotating metal plate over the holes near the bottom of the drum to control the amount of air coming in. The more air, the hotter the fire will burn.
2. Chimney: Attach a damper on the chimney or exhaust pipe to control how much smoke and heat escapes from the smoker. Adjusting this damper allows you to fine-tune the cooking temperature.

Step 5: Attach the Lid

If your drum comes with a removable lid, you're already set. If not, you can fashion a lid from sheet metal or purchase one to fit the top of the drum. The lid should fit snugly to trap the smoke inside the chamber. Make sure there's a handle for easy removal and some form of ventilation (such as a hole with a cover) to allow for smoke release when needed.

Step 6: Install a Temperature Gauge

Drill a small hole in the side of the smoker, just above the cooking grate, and install a temperature gauge. Monitoring the internal temperature is essential for proper smoking, allowing you to adjust the heat as needed.

Step 7: Paint (Optional)

If you want your smoker to be more durable and resistant to the elements, consider painting it with heat-resistant paint. This helps protect the metal from rust and adds a polished look to your smoker.

Step 8: Test and Season the Smoker

Before cooking any food, you'll need to season the smoker. This process helps burn off any remaining residues and prepares the metal to absorb and retain heat and smoke properly.

1. Build a Fire: Light a small fire in the charcoal basket using wood or lump charcoal. Close the lid and allow the smoker to heat up.
2. Run the Smoker: Let the smoker run for several hours, adjusting the airflow to keep the temperature stable. You can add some wood chunks to generate smoke and season the inside of the smoker.

Step 9: Start Smoking

Once your smoker is seasoned and ready, it's time to start cooking! Use hardwoods like hickory, mesquite, apple, or cherry for smoking, depending on the flavor you want. Fill the charcoal basket with a mix of charcoal and wood chunks, place your food on the grates, and maintain the temperature by adjusting the airflow.

Smoke meats like brisket, ribs, or chicken low and slow, checking your temperature gauge regularly to ensure consistent heat. The longer the cook time, the more tender and flavorful your food will be.

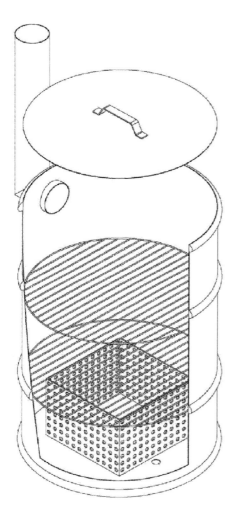
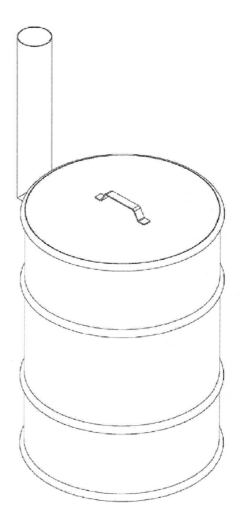

Wood Smoker

Building a smoker out of wood is a fun and rewarding project that can give your food that perfect smoky flavor. Unlike metal smokers, a wooden smoker adds an authentic, rustic feel to your cooking experience, and if done right, it can be a durable and effective way to smoke meats, fish, and veggies. Follow these steps to build a wooden smoker that's both functional and stylish.

Step 1: Choose Your Wood

Before you begin, select the right type of wood for building your smoker. Cedar, oak, and pine are popular choices because they are sturdy and resist decay. Cedar is particularly great because it withstands moisture and high temperatures, which are important factors for any smoker. Make sure the wood you choose is untreated, as treated wood can release harmful chemicals when exposed to heat.

Step 2: Gather Your Materials

For a basic vertical wooden smoker, you'll need:

- Wood planks (cedar or oak) for the walls
- Plywood or wood panels for the roof
- Wood screws or nails
- Metal hinges (for the door)
- Metal racks or grates for cooking surfaces
- Charcoal tray or firebox (can be bought or made from metal sheets)
- Chimney pipe or vents for smoke control
- Door latch
- Drill and saw for cutting and assembling the wood
- Thermometer to monitor the temperature inside

Step 3: Plan Your Smoker Design

A vertical box-style smoker is one of the easiest wooden smokers to build. It's essentially a large wooden box with multiple shelves for cooking and a firebox at the bottom. The firebox generates smoke and heat that circulates around the food inside the chamber. The overall dimensions depend on how much space you have and how much food you want to smoke, but a common size is around 3-4 feet tall and 2 feet wide.

Step 4: Build the Frame and Walls

1. Cut the wood planks to your desired dimensions. You'll need enough planks to build four walls, a door, and a roof. If you're going with a 3-foot tall smoker, cut the side panels to 3 feet and the width of the front and back walls to 2 feet.
2. Assemble the frame by screwing or nailing the wood planks together. Start with the back panel, then attach the side panels, and finally, add the front frame. Ensure that the wood panels fit snugly together to prevent smoke from leaking out.
3. Build the door by cutting a rectangular opening in the front wall for access to the smoker's interior. This opening will allow you to add food and tend the fire. Cut another piece of wood to fit this opening as the door and attach it to the frame with metal hinges.
4. Install a roof to keep the rain out and trap the heat and smoke. Cut a piece of plywood or wood panel that fits over the top of the smoker and attach it securely.

Step 5: Add Cooking Racks

Inside the smoker, you'll need shelves or racks to hold the food.

1. Install brackets or wood supports along the inside walls, spaced about 6-8 inches apart vertically, so you can place multiple racks at different levels.
2. Use metal racks or grates (stainless steel is best) to hold your food. These can be salvaged from old grills or purchased. Make sure the racks are strong enough to hold heavy cuts of meat.

Step 6: Build the Firebox

The firebox is where you'll generate the heat and smoke for your food. It needs to sit at the bottom of the smoker, slightly elevated to allow airflow.

1. You can build a simple firebox from metal sheets or use a metal tray. This tray should be wide enough to hold charcoal or wood chunks but small enough to fit inside the base of the smoker.
2. If possible, drill or cut small holes in the firebox to allow for better airflow. This will help regulate the fire and maintain a consistent temperature.
3. Elevate the firebox slightly off the bottom of the smoker using bricks or metal legs to ensure proper ventilation underneath the fire.

Step 7: Install Ventilation

Proper ventilation is critical for controlling the temperature and smoke levels inside your smoker.

1. Install a chimney or pipe at the top of the smoker. This will help release smoke and prevent the build-up of too much heat. A metal exhaust pipe or even a dryer vent pipe can work well. Attach the chimney securely to the roof of the smoker.
2. You'll also need air intake vents near the bottom of the smoker to feed the fire with oxygen. Drill a few holes on the sides near the base or install a sliding vent that you can open and close to regulate airflow.

Step 8: Add a Door Latch and Thermometer

1. Attach a latch to the door to ensure it stays closed during smoking, keeping the heat and smoke contained.
2. Drill a small hole in the front of the smoker, just above the cooking racks, and install a thermometer. This allows you to monitor the internal temperature and adjust the fire or vents as needed.

Step 9: Season Your Smoker

Before cooking, you'll need to season the smoker. This helps remove any impurities from the wood and preps it for cooking.

1. Light a small fire in the firebox using wood chunks or charcoal, and let the smoker heat up to around 250°F.
2. Let it burn for several hours, allowing the smoke to coat the interior. This will cure the wood and give the smoker its characteristic smell and flavor. You can also add some wood chips to create that rich smoky aroma.

Now that your wooden smoker is built and seasoned, you're ready to get smoking! Place your food on the racks, fire up the firebox with your favorite wood (hickory, applewood, or mesquite), and maintain a steady low temperature around 225°F-250°F. Keep an eye on the vents to control the airflow and smoke levels, and let your food absorb the rich, smoky flavor for several hours.

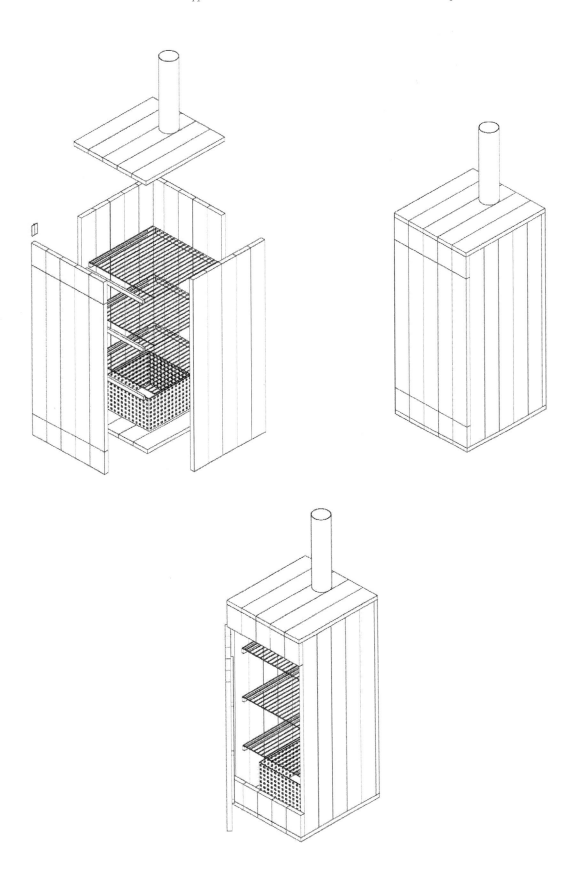

PART TWO

SURVIVAL SKILLS

CHAPTER 7

THE VITAL IMPORTANCE OF CLEAN DRINKING WATER

Drinking untreated water can expose you to a host of bacteria and parasites, leading to serious illness. The consequences can be severe, and it's crucial to understand the potential risks. But how do these diseases find their way into water sources? In both wilderness areas and regions with poor sanitation, water can easily become contaminated by human and animal activity. Whether it's from bathing, defecating, or even decomposing remains, the waste from humans and animals often makes its way into lakes, rivers, and streams, carrying harmful pathogens with it.

In the wilderness of the U.S., one of the most common waterborne illnesses is giardiasis, caused by a protozoan parasite. This nasty bug can lead to severe cramping and, worst of all, in any outdoor scenario, violent diarrhea—an affliction that can be especially dangerous when you're far from medical help.

But giardiasis isn't the only threat. Across the world's wilds, other waterborne diseases like dysentery, cholera, and various worms, viruses, and bacterial infections also lurk in untreated water. The symptoms of these illnesses often mirror those of giardiasis, with debilitating intestinal issues being the most common. In a survival situation, or even after a few days of strenuous hiking, diarrhea can exacerbate dehydration and put your life at serious risk. Protecting yourself from these dangers by treating all water before drinking is essential.

In any survival scenario, water is not just a necessity; it's your lifeline. Mastering the skills to locate, purify, store, and conserve water is paramount. Being prepared not only safeguards your health but also empowers you to face the unpredictable challenges of a doomsday situation with resilience and confidence.

In a doomsday scenario, clean drinking water is not just a resource; it's the bedrock of survival. It ensures that you stay hydrated, healthy, and strong, capable of facing the myriad challenges of a world turned upside down. It's the key to maintaining mental clarity, managing resources, and sustaining communities. Ultimately, those with access to clean water will likely endure and thrive amidst the chaos. So, as you prepare for the worst, remember that securing clean drinking water should be at the top of your list. Water will be the lifeline that will keep you going when everything else falls apart.

Drinking untreated water can expose you to a host of bacteria and parasites, leading to serious illness. The consequences can be severe, and it's crucial to understand the potential risks. But how do these diseases find their way into water sources? In both wilderness areas and regions with poor sanitation, water can easily become contaminated by human and animal activity. Whether it's from bathing, defecating, or even decomposing remains, the waste from humans and animals often makes its way into lakes, rivers, and streams, carrying harmful pathogens with it.

In the wilderness of the U.S., one of the most common waterborne illnesses is giardiasis, caused by a protozoan parasite. This nasty bug can lead to severe cramping and, worst of all, in any outdoor scenario, violent diarrhea—an affliction that can be especially dangerous when you're far from medical help.

But giardiasis isn't the only threat. Across the world's wilds, other waterborne diseases like dysentery, cholera, and various worms, viruses, and bacterial infections also lurk in untreated water. The symptoms of these illnesses often mirror those of giardiasis, with debilitating intestinal issues being the most common. In a survival situation, or even after a few days of strenuous hiking, diarrhea can exacerbate dehydration and put your life at serious risk. Protecting yourself from these dangers by treating all water before drinking is essential.

Water filtration and purification are two critical processes for making water safe to drink, but they serve different purposes—and knowing the difference can be a lifesaver.

Water Filtration is the first line of defense. It involves passing water through a cloth, mesh net, or commercial filter to remove debris and some bacteria. Think of it as a sieve that strains out the larger particles and impurities. However, while filters can catch protozoa and bacteria, they're not foolproof—they can't stop viruses, which are too small to be trapped by the mesh. A good filter is usually enough if you're backpacking in the U.S. or Canada, especially in mountainous regions. These areas generally have water sources that are considered safe for filtration-only methods. But be cautious—many cases of illness on the trail aren't from the water itself but from poor sanitation practices, like not washing hands or improper waste disposal.

Additionally, filtration ensures your water tastes fresh and natural, without the chemical aftertaste that can come with some purification methods. Plus, you can drink it immediately, with no waiting time. But remember, while filtration can make your water look and taste clean, it doesn't guarantee complete safety. If a virus lurks in that water, a filter won't catch it, and the consequences could be severe.

Water purification is about making water safe to drink by neutralizing all harmful pathogens, including those sneaky viruses that filtration misses. Purification doesn't remove debris or dirt, so you should always filter first. You can achieve purification through boiling, chemical treatments, or UV light exposure, and it's especially crucial when traveling in areas where waterborne viruses are a real threat, such as in less-developed regions of the world.

Boiling water for at least one minute is the most reliable method, as it kills all pathogens. Chemical agents like iodine or chlorine are also effective, though they can leave an unpleasant taste and require waiting before the water is safe to drink. UV purifiers are quick and efficient but require batteries, solar power, and clear water to work correctly.

The bottom line is that while water filtration makes your water cleaner and tastier, it doesn't make it completely safe. Water purification is essential to eliminating all potential threats, especially when you're in an environment where viruses are a concern. Sometimes, you'll need to use both methods to ensure your water is not only clear of debris but also free of harmful pathogens. In the wild, understanding when to filter and when to purify could be the difference between staying healthy and facing a potentially life-threatening illness.

Methods for Water Filtration and Purification

When it comes to making water safe to drink in the wild, understanding the right methods for filtration and purification is crucial. Below, we'll dive into some of the most common techniques, along with their pros and cons.

DIY Filters

DIY water filters are a last-resort option, meant for survival scenarios when no other means are available. These methods are not something you should rely on for planned camping trips. Ideally, after using a DIY filter, you should still purify the water by boiling it or using purification tablets.

- Rock/Sand Layer Cake: This classic wilderness filter involves layering various materials like sand, pebbles, and charcoal in a hollow log, bag, or even a piece of cloth. Water drips down through the layers, filtering out impurities. While this method can remove some bacteria and debris, it's not foolproof—many harmful pathogens may still slip through.

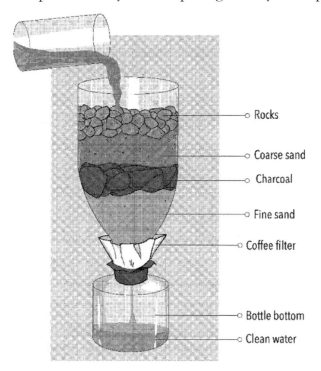

- Shirt/Cloth: Passing water through a cloth will remove dirt and debris but won't do much against bacteria or viruses. It's a basic step that improves water clarity, but it's crucial to purify afterward.
- Container Sedimentation: If you have no other options, place muddy or dirty water in a container and let it stand for 12 hours. The sediment will settle at the bottom, leaving clearer water on top. However, this does nothing to remove harmful pathogens, so it's far from a complete solution.

Commercial Filters

Commercial filters offer more reliable water filtration and, in some cases, purification.

- Survival Straws: Products like LifeStraw have gained popularity for their convenience. You can drink directly from a water source using the straw, which filters out bacteria and protozoa. However, most survival straws don't filter out viruses, so they're best used in regions like the U.S. or Canada where viral contamination is less of a concern. Straws can be pricey up front, but they're cost-effective in the long run, filtering up to 1,000 liters of water.
- Pump/Gravity Filters: These systems are more comprehensive, often combining filtration with purification. Many use ceramic filters to remove larger pathogens and silver to deactivate viruses. Pump filters work quickly but require manual effort, while gravity filters are slower but require no power source. They're bulkier and pricier than other options, but their reliability in a variety of scenarios makes them a good investment.

Boiling

Boiling is the gold standard for water purification. According to the EPA, a rolling boil for one minute will kill all harmful pathogens, including viruses. At altitudes above 5,000 feet, boil for three minutes. The downside is that boiling requires a fire and fuel, which might not always be available. Additionally, boiling leads to some water loss through evaporation—a concern when every drop counts.

Chemical Purification (Iodine/Chlorine/Bleach)

Chemical treatments are a portable and effective way to purify water, especially when boiling isn't an option.

- Iodine: Add 5 drops of a 2% iodine tincture per quart of water (10 drops if the water is cloudy). Wait 30 minutes before drinking. Iodine is compact and multipurpose, but it imparts a noticeable taste to the water and isn't safe for everyone, particularly pregnant women and those with shellfish allergies.
- Chlorine: Chlorine tablets take about 4 hours to purify water and are effective against most pathogens. They have a longer shelf life and leave less of an aftertaste compared to iodine.
- Bleach: In urban emergencies, household bleach can be used to purify water. Ensure it contains 5-8% sodium hypochlorite, and use 2 drops per quart of water, waiting 30 minutes before drinking. Bleach should be a last resort, as it's less convenient to carry in the wilderness.

UV/Solar Purification

- SODIS (Solar Water Disinfection): This method relies on UV rays from the sun to kill bacteria and microorganisms. Fill a clear plastic bottle with water and leave it in direct sunlight for 12-48 hours. It's a simple, equipment-free option but should be used as a last resort since it may not eliminate all pathogens.
- UV Devices: These gadgets emit UV light to neutralize harmful organisms. They're effective against bacteria and viruses but require batteries or a hand crank to operate. Since they don't filter out debris, it's best to pre-filter water before using a UV device.

Bottom Line: Choosing the Right Method for Various Scenarios

- For Hiking/Backpacking in First-World Countries: In places like the U.S. and Canada, where groundwater is usually free of viruses, a good commercial filter or survival straw will generally suffice. Chemical treatments are also a lightweight option for long treks.
- For International Travel: When venturing into less-developed regions, combine filtration with purification to protect against all potential pathogens. Tablets, UV devices, or filters with purification capabilities are essential.

- For Wilderness Survival: In an emergency where you're stranded, and commercial options aren't available, boiling is your safest bet if you have fuel and water. If not, DIY filters or sedimentation methods can reduce risk, but purification should follow whenever possible.

Remember: Filtration improves water clarity and removes debris, but purification is what makes water truly safe to drink. In any survival situation, it's better to drink untreated water than to risk dehydration but knowing how to make water safer is always your best line of defense.

Rainwater Collection

Collecting rainwater is an effective way to conserve water and make use of a free natural resource. Here's a guide to setting up an efficient rainwater harvesting system:

Materials: Rain barrels or large storage tanks, Downspout diverter or rainwater filter, Gutters and downspouts, flush diverter, Mesh screen or leaf guard, Faucet or spigot, Overflow pipe, and Platform or stand (optional)

Tools Needed: Ladder, Drill, Saw, Screwdriver, Level, Measuring tape

Step-by-Step Guide:

1. Choose and Prepare the Collection Area: Select a Location: Choose a location with a large roof area to maximize rainwater collection. The location should be near where you intend to use the water. Clean the Roof and Gutters: Ensure the roof and gutters are clean and free of debris. Install a leaf guard or mesh screen on the gutters to keep leaves and large debris out.

2. Install Gutters and Downspouts: Attach Gutters: Install gutters along the edges of the roof where water naturally flows. Make sure the gutters slope slightly toward the downspout to facilitate water flow. Install Downspouts: Attach downspouts to the gutters to direct the water to your collection system. Position the downspouts so that they lead to your rain barrels or storage tanks.

3. Set Up the Rain Barrels or Storage Tanks: Choose Storage Containers: Select rain barrels or larger storage tanks depending on your water needs. Food-grade plastic barrels are a good option. Position the Barrels: Place the barrels or tanks on a stable, elevated platform if possible. Elevation will help with water pressure when using the water. Install a Spigot: Attach a faucet or spigot near the bottom of the barrel for easy water access. Drill a hole and use a bulkhead fitting to ensure it is watertight.

4. Connect the Downspouts: Downspout Diverter: Install a downspout diverter to direct water from the downspout into the barrel. The diverter can be a commercial product or a homemade setup. First Flush Diverter: Install a first flush diverter to discard the initial flow of rainwater, which may contain contaminants from the roof. This ensures cleaner water enters your storage system.

5. Overflow and Maintenance: Overflow Pipe: Install an overflow pipe near the top of the barrel to handle excess water. Direct the overflow away from the foundation of your house to prevent damage. Inspect and Clean: Regularly inspect and clean the gutters, downspouts, and barrels to ensure the system works efficiently and the water remains clean.

6. Using the Collected Water: Watering Plants: Use the collected rainwater for irrigation. Attach a hose to the spigot or use a watering can. Household Use: With proper filtration and treatment, rainwater can be used for non-potable household purposes such as flushing toilets or washing clothes.

7. Additional Considerations: Filtration and Purification: If you plan to use the water for drinking, ensure it undergoes appropriate filtration and purification processes to remove contaminants.

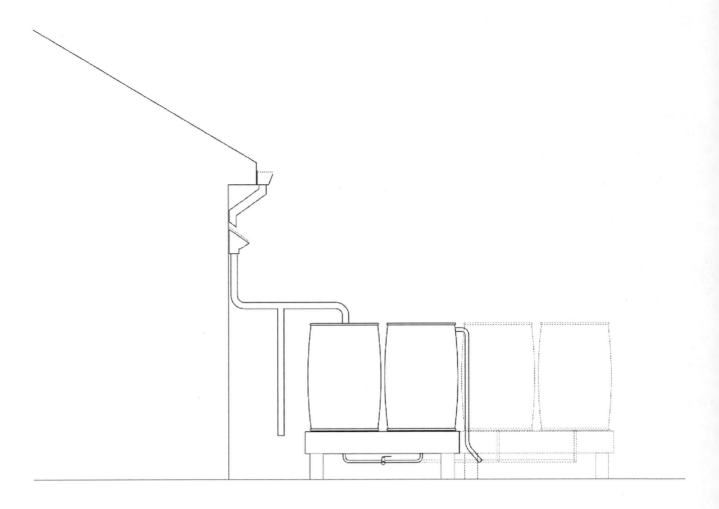

Seasonal Adjustments: In colder climates, ensure your system is prepared for winter. Drain and store the barrels or use materials that can withstand freezing temperatures.

By following these steps, you can set up an efficient rainwater harvesting system to conserve water and make the most of natural rainfall. Regular maintenance and monitoring will help ensure the system remains effective and the water quality is maintained.

Digging a well in an emergency situation requires a simplified approach, focusing on essential steps to access water quickly. Here's a streamlined guide to help you dig a basic emergency well:

Materials: Shovel or digging tools

Buckets and rope (for removing soil and water)

Gravel and sand (optional for basic filtration)

Well casing (PVC pipe or similar)

Well screen (or a makeshift version using a fine mesh)

Rope or chain (for safety)

Water container for collecting water.

Tools Needed: Shovel or spade, Post hole digger or auger (if available), Saw (if you need to cut the casing), Measuring tape

Step-by-Step Guide:

1. Site Selection: Choose a Low Point: Select a location at a lower elevation where water is more likely to be found. Away from Contaminants: Ensure the site is at least 100 feet away from potential contaminants like septic tanks or latrines.

2. Digging the Well: Start with a Pilot Hole: Begin by digging a small pilot hole using a shovel or post hole digger. Aim for a diameter of about 2-3 feet. Deepen the Hole: Continue digging deeper until you reach the water table. Depth will vary, but even a shallow well of 10-15 feet may yield water in some areas. Remove Soil: Use buckets to remove soil and periodically check for moisture indicating proximity to the water table.

3. Well Casing: Insert the Casing: If available, insert a PVC pipe or similar material into the hole to prevent the walls from collapsing and to keep the water clean. Cut to Fit: Cut the casing to fit the depth of your well, ensuring it extends a bit above ground level. Seal Around the Casing: Use gravel around the outside of the casing to provide some basic filtration and stability.

4. Creating a Makeshift Well Screen: Simple Mesh Screen: If a proper well screen isn't available, use a fine mesh or cloth secured over the bottom of the casing to filter out sediments. Attach Securely: Ensure the makeshift screen is securely attached to prevent it from detaching and contaminating the well.

5. Develop the Well: Bail Out Dirty Water: Use a bucket to remove any dirty water and debris from the well. This may take several attempts to clear out the murky water and allow clean water to flow in. Basic Disinfection: If possible, add a small amount of chlorine bleach (a few tablespoons) to disinfect the well. Let it sit for a few hours and then bail out the water.

6. Safety and Collection: Use a rope or chain to lower a container into the well to collect water. Ensure the rope or chain is strong and securely tied. If available, a manual hand pump can make accessing water easier and more efficient.

Monitor Water Quality: Regularly check the water for clarity and any signs of contamination. Always boil or filter the water before use if possible.

Additional Tips: Stay Safe: Always prioritize safety. Ensure the well is stable and avoid digging too deep too quickly to prevent collapse.

Use Resources Wisely: In an emergency, improvising with available materials is key. Be resourceful with what you have.

By following these steps, you can create a basic emergency well to access water quickly. Regular maintenance and monitoring are essential to ensure the well remains functional and the water safe to use.

CHAPTER 8

THE POWER OF FIRE

Knowing how to build a fire is one of the most important survival skills you can possess, and it goes far beyond simply staying warm. Fire is your lifeline in the wild, serving as your primary defense against the cold. In harsh conditions, hypothermia can set in faster than you might expect when your body loses heat rapidly. A well-built fire provides the warmth needed to dry wet clothes and maintain your core body temperature, making it crucial for survival.

Beyond warmth, fire is the key to cooking and nutrition. Raw food in the wild can be unsafe and difficult to digest, but with fire, you can cook your meals, making them safer and easier to digest. Cooking also kills harmful bacteria and parasites, ensuring you get the calories and nutrients necessary to maintain energy levels.

Water, another critical element of survival, often needs to be purified in the wild. Many water sources can be contaminated, and drinking untreated water can lead to serious illness. By building a fire, you can boil water, killing pathogens and making it safe to drink. This is essential for staying hydrated and avoiding waterborne diseases.

If you find yourself lost or stranded, a fire becomes a powerful tool for signaling for help. During the day, the smoke is visible from afar, while at night, the flames can attract attention. A well-maintained fire increases your chances of being found by rescuers.

Fire also protects against predators. Most wild animals are naturally wary of fire, and its presence creates a barrier that keeps you safer as you rest or sleep. When darkness falls, the fire provides light, preventing you from injuring yourself by stumbling in the dark. It also gives you a sense of security, allowing you to manage your surroundings confidently.

The psychological benefits of a fire are immense. The flame's warmth, light, and comforting crackle can lift your spirits in a stressful or frightening situation. This boost in morale is critical for maintaining a positive mindset and the will to survive.

Fire also enables the creation of tools and craft necessities. You can harden the tips of wooden spears, mold materials, and even use the smoke to create signals. Additionally, the smoke from a fire acts as an insect repellent, keeping annoying and potentially harmful insects at bay, which is especially crucial in areas with high pest activity.

Lastly, knowing how to build a fire builds confidence and self-reliance. It teaches you that you have the skills to handle unexpected situations and take care of yourself in the wilderness. Mastering the art of building a fire is not just about acquiring a survival skill; it's about ensuring your safety, health, and well-being in any situation where you might be vulnerable. Whether you're camping, hiking, or facing a true survival scenario, the ability to build a fire could very well save your life.

Here are three effective methods to start a fire:

Matches or Lighter

Using matches or a lighter is the most straightforward method to start a fire. Materials: Matches or lighter, Tinder (dry leaves, pine needles, paper), Kindling (small sticks), Firewood. Steps:

1. Prepare the Fire Site: Clear a space that's safe for a fire, ensuring it's free from overhanging branches and away from tents and structures. You can use a fire ring or create a circle of rocks.
2. Build a Tinder Nest: Place your tinder in the center of your fire site. This material needs to catch fire easily and burn fast.
3. Add Kindling: Arrange the kindling over the tinder in a teepee or lean-to structure, allowing for airflow.
4. Light the Tinder: Light the tinder with your matches or lighter. As the tinder begins to burn, the kindling will catch.
5. Gradually Add Firewood: Once the kindling is burning well, start adding larger pieces of firewood, being careful not to smother the flames.

Ferro Rod (Fire Steel)

A ferrocerium rod is durable and works even when wet, making it ideal for rugged outdoor conditions. Materials: Ferro rod, Striker or knife, Tinder, Kindling, and Firewood

Steps:

1. Prepare Your Tinder: Create a dense nest of tinder that will easily catch sparks.
2. Position the Ferro Rod: Hold the ferro rod close to the tinder and angle the striker or the back of a knife blade to scrape down the rod swiftly.
3. Spark It: Use a quick, strong motion to scrape the rod, directing the sparks into the tinder.
4. Build the Fire: Once the tinder catches, proceed as above by adding kindling and then firewood to build your fire.

Bow Drill

The bow drill method is a traditional technique that requires more skill and patience but can be highly effective in survival situations.

Materials:

Bow (curved stick with a cord)

Spindle (straight, round stick)

Fireboard (flat piece of wood with a notch)

Socket (stone or wood to hold the top of the spindle)

Tinder

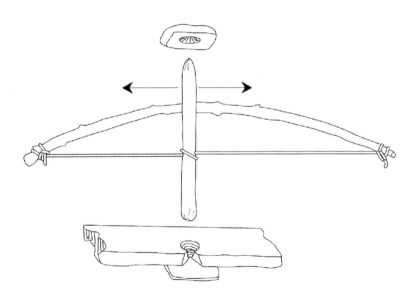

Steps:

1. Prepare the Fireboard: Cut a small depression in the fireboard and a notch connecting to the edge of the board.
2. Set Up the Bow Drill: Wrap the bow's cord around the spindle once. Place one end of the spindle in the fireboard's depression and the other end in the socket held in your hand.
3. Start Drilling: Use one hand to hold the socket and the other to move the bow back and forth. This action will rotate the spindle, generating friction and heat on the fireboard.

4. Catch the Ember: As you drill, an ember will form in the fireboard notch. Once visible, carefully transfer this ember to a tinder nest.

5. Ignite the Tinder: Gently blow on the ember within the tinder until it ignites, then build up your fire with kindling and firewood.

Each method has its strengths and situations where it performs best. Whether using modern tools like matches or traditional methods like a bow drill, the key to successful fire-starting is practice and preparation.

Critical safety warning: Always extinguish your campfire completely before going to sleep. Numerous accidents have occurred due to a sudden gust of wind in the night that can easily scatter embers onto tents or dry grass, igniting a dangerous fire. Never underestimate the risk; a few moments of caution can prevent a potentially life-threatening situation.

To stay warm through the long hours of night, consider burying fire-warmed stones beneath your sleeping bag. The hot stones with warm the ground beneath you for hours and you can rest easy knowing your fire is out.

Smokeless Fire

Creating a smokeless fire is highly beneficial for minimizing detection in survival situations, reducing environmental impact, or simply enhancing the enjoyment of a campfire by avoiding heavy smoke. Here are steps and tips for building a fire that produces minimal smoke:

Materials:

Dry, seasoned wood (hardwoods are best)

Tinder (dry leaves, paper, small twigs)

Kindling (small sticks)

Larger firewood

Tips for to Building a Smokeless Fire:

1. Select the Right Fuel: - Choose Dry Wood: The key to a smokeless fire is using wood that is thoroughly dry and well-seasoned. Moisture in the wood causes smoke, so dry wood is essential. Hardwoods like oak, maple, and birch burn longer and cleaner than softwoods, producing less smoke.

2. Prepare the Fire Site: Choose a location shielded from wind but still well-ventilated. Clear any debris and create a small pit or use a fire ring to contain the fire.

3. Create a Good Foundation: Lay a flat bed of hardwood logs close together at the bottom of your fire site. This dense base will facilitate a more complete combustion of the wood, reducing smoke.

4. Build the Fire Structure: Teepee Structure: Place your tinder in the center and build a teepee of kindling around it. Then, layer smaller pieces of hardwood around the kindling, followed by progressively larger pieces as you build up.

Top-Down (Upside Down) Fire: Start with larger logs at the bottom laid out parallel. Then layer smaller logs, followed by kindling and finally tinder at the top. This method will burn down from the top, heating the logs below and creating a hotter, more efficient fire that burns, more of the gases released from the wood.

5. Light the Fire: Ignite the tinder. If using the top-down method, the fire will start from the top and slowly burn downwards, requiring less tending and producing less smoke as the heat preheats the wood below, releasing gases that then burn off more completely.

6. Maintain Properly: Keep the fire moderate in size; a larger fire might produce more smoke. Manage the fire by adding more wood as needed but allow each piece to burn completely before adding more.

7. Ensure Complete Combustion: Good combustion is key to a smokeless fire. Ensure the fire is hot enough so that the wood gases are incinerated rather than released into the air.

Additional Tips:

Avoid Green Wood: Freshly cut or green wood contains a lot of moisture, which leads to smoke. Airflow is Crucial: Make sure there is adequate airflow; a fire that is choked or stifled will smoke heavily.

No Overcrowding: Don't overcrowd your fire with too much wood, as this reduces the airflow and increases smoke production. Building a smokeless fire takes practice and attention to detail, especially in selecting and preparing the wood.

By following these steps, you can achieve a cleaner, more efficient fire that minimizes smoke and maximizes warmth and light. Starting a fire is a fundamental skill, especially for camping, survival situations, or just enjoying a backyard bonfire.

Five Popular Types of Outdoor Cooking:

1. Grilling:

One of the most common methods, grilling involves cooking food on a grill over charcoal, wood, or gas. It's perfect for meats, vegetables, and even some fruits, providing a distinctive charred flavor.

2. Barbecuing

Often confused with grilling, barbecuing is a slower process that uses lower temperatures and longer cooking times. Food is typically cooked over indirect heat with the addition of wood smoke for flavoring, making it ideal for tougher cuts of meat that become tender and flavorful.

3. Open Fire Cooking

This primal method involves cooking directly over an open flame. It can include grilling on a grate, roasting on sticks, or even placing pots and pans over the fire. Open fire cooking imparts a smoky flavor and requires skill in managing heat.

4. Dutch Oven Cooking

A Dutch oven is a thick-walled cooking pot with a tight-fitting lid, ideal for outdoor use. It's versatile for baking, stewing, frying, and roasting. Dutch ovens can be placed directly into a campfire or on top of coals, allowing for a range of dishes from stews to bread and cakes.

5. Smoking

Smoking is a method of flavoring, cooking, or preserving food by exposing it to smoke from burning or smoldering material, typically wood. Different woods impart different flavors, and the low and slow cooking process is great for enhancing the flavor of meats and fish. Each method offers a different experience and outcome, often influenced by the type of fuel used and the cook's ability to control the heat.

Outdoor cooking is not just about the food; it's also about enjoying the outdoors and mastering the elements. Cooking directly with fire can be a rewarding and enjoyable experience, especially outdoors.

Here are five ways to cook using just fire:

1. Direct Grilling

This involves placing food directly over the flame or coals on a grill. It's great for quickly cooking items like steaks, burgers, vegetables, and small cuts of meat, providing them with a charred and smoky flavor.

2. Skewering

Food can be skewered on sticks or metal skewers and held over the flames. This method is excellent for cooking items like kebabs, sausages, marshmallows, and even bread dough. It allows for even cooking by rotating the skewers.

3. Spit Roasting

Larger cuts of meat or whole animals can be cooked using a spit, which is a long rod used to hold food while it rotates over a fire. This method allows heat to distribute evenly, slowly cooking the meat to perfection over several hours.

4. Pit Cooking

This ancient technique involves digging a pit, heating stones in a fire, placing the food either directly on the stones or in containers, and then covering it with earth to cook for several hours. It's ideal for large gatherings and can be used to cook whole animals, vegetables, or wrapped food packets.

5. Ash Cooking

Food such as potatoes, onions, or even fish can be wrapped in leaves or foil and placed directly into hot ashes at the edge of a fire. The ash provides insulation and a gentle, even heat, cooking the food through in its own moisture. Each of these methods uses fire in a unique way to impart flavors that can't be replicated with modern cooking appliances. Plus, cooking with fire is a skill that connects you with nature and history, offering a deeply satisfying culinary experience.

Cooking without gas or electricity can be an enjoyable and rewarding experience, especially if you're camping, dealing with a power outage, or simply looking to reduce your carbon footprint.

Here are several methods you can use to cook food without relying on modern utilities:

1. Solar Cooking: Utilize a solar cooker or solar oven, which harnesses sunlight to heat and cook food. These devices can bake, roast, and steam, provided there is sufficient sunlight. They're environmentally friendly and perfect for sunny days.

2. Wood Fire Cooking: Create a fire using wood logs or branches in a safe outdoor area. You can cook directly over the flames, use a grill grate, or employ a Dutch oven or other fire-safe cookware to prepare your meals.

3. Charcoal Grill: Use a charcoal grill for both direct and indirect cooking. Charcoal provides a steady and controllable heat source, ideal for grilling meats, vegetables, and even for slow-cooking and smoking.

4. Alcohol and Gel Fuel Stoves: Small and portable, these stoves use alcohol or gel-based fuels to create a flame. They are great for camping or emergency cooking, suitable for boiling water and cooking simple meals.

5. Biofuel Cookers: These devices use organic materials such as wood pellets, dried animal dung, or compressed biomass as fuel. They are often used in outdoor settings or in parts of the world where other fuel sources are scarce.

6. Rocket Stove: A rocket stove uses small pieces of biomass like twigs and leaves, efficiently burning them at high temperatures due to its insulated design. It's excellent for boiling and simmering. Each method has its unique advantages and is suitable for different settings and needs. Whether you're cooking for fun or out of necessity, these techniques ensure that you can prepare food even without conventional utilities.

DIY Outdoor Oven

Building an outdoor oven can be a rewarding project that enhances your cooking capabilities and outdoor entertainment area. Here's a basic guide on how to construct a simple outdoor wood-fired oven <u>before</u> disaster strikes:

Materials:
- Firebricks or refractory bricks
- Clay or refractory cement
- Sand
- Concrete blocks or cinder blocks (for the base)
- Metal rebar or wire mesh (for reinforcement)
- Heat-resistant mortar
- Ceramic fiber blanket (for insulation)
- Gravel
- Wooden boards (for formwork)

Tools:
- Shovel
- Trowel
- Wheelbarrow (for mixing concrete)
- Spirit level
- Measuring tape

Steps:
1. Design and Planning: Decide on the size and location of your oven. Ensure the location is safe and away from any flammable structures. Sketch out your design. Typical outdoor ovens have a dome shape with a front opening.

2. Prepare the Foundation: Dig a foundation about 5-6 inches deep and fill it with a layer of gravel for drainage. Pour a concrete slab (about 4 inches thick) over the gravel. Reinforce with wire mesh or rebar. Allow the concrete to cure for several days.

3. Construct the Base: Build a base using concrete blocks or bricks to your desired height, typically around 36 inches. Fill the blocks with concrete for stability. Create a flat cooking surface on top of the base using firebricks. Lay them closely together to form the oven floor.

4. Build the Dome: Construct a sand mold to help form the shape of the dome or use a pre-made form. Start laying your firebricks or clay around the form to create the dome. Use heat-resistant mortar to secure the bricks. Ensure the front opening (where you will place and remove food) is properly sized and shaped.

5. Insulate the Dome: Once the dome is complete and the mortar has set, cover it with a layer of ceramic fiber blanket to insulate. Apply a layer of refractory cement or clay over the insulation for additional protection and heat retention.

6. Chimney Installation: Install a chimney at the front part of the dome, just above the oven opening. This helps in drawing smoke out of the oven.

7. Curing the Oven: Once you've removed the sand, gradually heat the oven with small fires to cure the clay or cement. This reduces moisture inside the materials and prevents cracking. Increase the size of the fires over several days until the oven is fully cured.

8. Finishing Touches: Optionally, you can plaster the outside or add tiles for aesthetic purposes and extra insulation. Install a door to cover the opening when the oven is not in use to maintain and maximize heat retention.

Safety Tips: Ensure the oven is stable and sturdy. Build in a well-ventilated area to avoid smoke inhalation. Always have fire extinguishing methods nearby in case of an emergency. Building an outdoor oven is a complex but enjoyable DIY project.

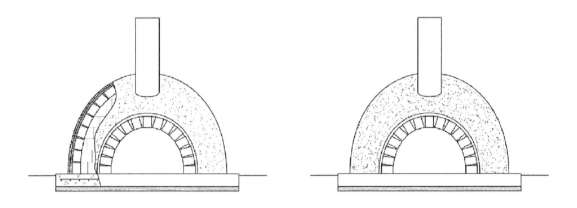

Take your time with each step to ensure safety and functionality. Enjoy the rustic and rich flavors of wood-fired cooking. Building a mud oven is a fun and sustainable project that utilizes natural materials to create a functional outdoor oven for baking and cooking.

Should emergencies arise, and you do not have access to your local home improvement store or electricity, here's a step-by-step guide on how to build your own mud oven with materials you could find in your own back yard:

Materials:

Clay soil (can be sourced locally or purchased)

Sand, Straw or dried grass, water, bricks or stones (for the base),

Wooden form (for shaping the oven entrance)

Tools: Shovel

Bucket or large container (for mixing)

Tarp (for mixing clay and sand)

Measuring tape

Level

Steps:

1. Select the Site: Choose a level site that's away from buildings and not under trees. It should be a spot that can handle fire and smoke.

2. Prepare the Foundation: Clear the area of any vegetation. Lay a circular foundation of bricks or stones approximately 3-5 feet in diameter. This will raise your oven off the ground and provide a stable, heat-resistant base.

3. Create the Oven Floor: On top of your foundation, lay a layer of sand to level the surface. Place firebricks or flat stones over the sand to form the oven floor. This is where your baking will occur, so it should be flat and even.

4. Mix Mud: Mix clay soil, sand, and water in roughly equal parts to form a malleable mud. Add straw to the mixture for additional strength. The straw acts as reinforcement. A common ratio is 1 part clay to 2 parts sand, but this can vary based on the clay's natural composition. Use a tarp to help mix these ingredients by placing them on the tarp and stomping them with your feet until the mixture is well combined and has the consistency of stiff dough.

5. Build the Dome: Form a dome-shaped mound of damp sand on the brick floor to act as a temporary form for your mud mixture. This should be the size and shape of the inside of your desired oven. Cover the sand form with newspaper. This prevents the mud from mixing with the sand when you later remove the sand. Apply the mud mixture over the newspaper-covered sand form. The walls should be about 4-6 inches thick. Smooth and compress the mud as you build up the layers.

6. Cover the wet mud with a tarp an allow to dry for several days. Once dry, gently scoop out the sand and spread around the perimeter of your oven. Once the oven is empty, build a fire within. The newspaper will burn away, and the clay will cure to withstand weather. When not in use, keeping your oven covered is ideal.

While cooking, bank the fire or coals toward the back of the oven and place the food you are cooking within. Turn your food frequently to be sure it cooks evenly.

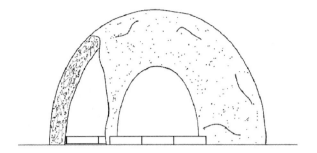 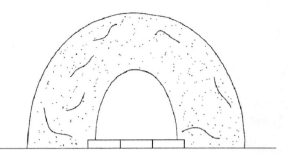

CHAPTER 9

GARDENING

Planning and Designing a Survival Garden

Creating a survival garden is a rewarding journey toward self-reliance, and it's more achievable than you might think! With thoughtful planning and a bit of dedication, you can build a garden that provides fresh, nutritious food in times of need. This chapter from the "PREPPER'S GARDENING GUIDE" offers the tools you need to plan and design a garden that will flourish and sustain you and your loved ones.

Vision and Strategy

- Space Assessment: Whether you're working with a backyard, a balcony, or a larger area, assess your space carefully. Look for spots that receive good sunlight and have quality soil.
- Defining Purpose: What will your garden provide? Fresh produce, medicinal herbs, or a combination? Define your purpose and stay focused on it.
- Crop Selection: Choose crops that thrive in your climate and are known for their high yield and long shelf life. The right selections will maximize your efforts.
- Companion Planting: Use companion planting to improve growth and naturally deter pests.
- Vertical Gardening: If space is limited, think up! Trellises and wall planters can help maximize your growing area.

Nurturing the Soil

Healthy soil is the key to a bountiful harvest:

- Soil Testing: Conduct a soil test to learn its pH and nutrient content. Adjust accordingly for optimal growth.
- Composting: Start a composting system to naturally enrich your soil over time.
- Mulching: Mulch helps retain moisture and suppress weeds, making it easier to maintain your garden.

Water Management

Water is life for your plants:

- Drip Irrigation: A drip system helps conserve water and ensures your plants get the hydration they need without waste.
- Rainwater Collection: Install a rain barrel to collect free water and use it during dry spells.

Seasonal Gardening

Work with the seasons for year-round production:

- Succession Planting: By planting in stages, you can enjoy a continuous harvest throughout the growing season.
- Winter Gardening: Don't let winter stop you! Explore cold-weather crops or invest in a greenhouse to keep your garden going year-round.

Pest and Disease Control

Keep your garden healthy and productive:

- Integrated Pest Management (IPM): Use a mix of prevention, beneficial insects, and natural remedies to keep pests at bay.
- Companion Plants: Certain plants naturally repel pests and attract beneficial insects—use them to your advantage!

Saving Seeds for the Future

Ensuring your garden's future:

- Open-Pollinated Varieties: Opt for open-pollinated plants so you can save seeds year after year.
- Seed Storage: Learn how to properly dry and store seeds to keep your garden thriving for seasons to come.

Garden Security and Community

Keep your garden safe and share its benefits with others:

- Fencing: A simple fence will protect your garden from wildlife or unwanted intruders.
- Community Collaboration: Share resources and ideas with neighbors or local gardening groups to grow a stronger, more resilient community.

Soil Preparation and Nutrient Management

Healthy soil is the foundation of your garden's success. By preparing and nurturing your soil, you'll create a space where plants can thrive.

Soil Assessment and Amendments

- Soil Testing: Start with a test to understand your soil's pH and nutrient needs.

- Organic Matter: Add compost or manure to improve the soil's structure and fertility.
- Nutrient Balance: Use organic fertilizers like bone meal or fish emulsion to ensure your plants get the nutrients they need.

Raised Beds and Containers

- Custom Soil Mix: For raised beds or containers, create a soil mix rich in compost and organic matter.
- Drainage: Ensure proper drainage to keep your plants healthy and prevent root rot.

Mulching and Crop Rotation

- Mulch: Mulch helps maintain moisture, suppress weeds, and regulate soil temperature.
- Crop Rotation: Rotate crops each year to prevent disease buildup and maintain soil health.

Selecting and Growing High-Yield Crops

Choosing the right crops is the secret to a thriving survival garden. Let's explore how to pick the best plants to ensure a steady and abundant harvest.

Crop Selection

- Climate Compatibility: Select crops that are suited to your climate and can withstand local pests.
- Nutrient-Rich Varieties: Choose crops that are not only high-yield but packed with nutrients like kale, spinach, and sweet potatoes.
- Storage Potential: Prioritize crops with long shelf lives, such as root vegetables, squash, and apples.

High-Yield Crops

- Leafy Greens: Fast-growing crops like lettuce and kale provide continuous harvests.
- Root Vegetables: Carrots, beets, and radishes are easy to grow and store well.
- Legumes: Beans and peas not only produce plentiful crops but also enrich your soil with nitrogen.
- Cucurbits: Zucchini, cucumbers, and squash are reliable, high-yield producers.

Crop Care Techniques

- Companion Planting: Maximize your garden's potential by pairing plants that boost each other's growth.
- Spacing and Pruning: Give your plants room to grow and prune regularly to focus their energy on fruit production.

Harvest and Preservation

- Timing: Harvest crops at their peak for the best flavor and nutrition.
- Preservation: Learn preservation methods like canning, freezing, and drying to extend the life of your harvest.
- Seed Saving: Save seeds from your best crops to ensure a thriving garden year after year.

With the right planning and a little hard work, your survival garden will become a reliable source of fresh food and a symbol of your self-sufficiency. You've got the tools, now it's time to get planting! Your journey toward self-reliance starts in your garden, and every step you take brings you closer to a bountiful harvest.

Seed Storage

Storing seeds properly is essential for maintaining their viability and ensuring successful germination in future planting seasons. To begin, always start with healthy, mature seeds harvested at the right time. Make sure the seeds have fully ripened before collecting them. Once harvested, allow the seeds to dry thoroughly by spreading them out on paper towels or a mesh screen in a cool, dry place for a week or two. This step is crucial as moisture can cause mold or premature germination.

Before storage, clean the seeds by removing any plant material, dirt, or pulp to prevent mold and enhance longevity. After cleaning, select an airtight container for storage. Glass jars, sealed plastic bags, or vacuum-sealed pouches are ideal for keeping out moisture and air, both of which can reduce seed viability. Glass jars with tight-fitting lids are particularly effective in protecting seeds from pests. Including a desiccant, like a silica gel packet or powdered milk wrapped in tissue, can help absorb any excess moisture inside the container, further preserving the seeds.

It's important to label each container with the type of seed and the date of storage. This helps track the age of the seeds and monitor their viability over time. For optimal storage, place the containers in a cool, dark, and dry environment. Seeds should ideally be stored at temperatures between 32°F and 50°F (0°C to 10°C). A refrigerator can be an excellent option, but ensure the seeds are in airtight containers to prevent moisture buildup from condensation. Keeping the seeds away from light and humidity will prevent them from deteriorating quickly.

To check if seeds are still viable after some time, conduct a germination test. Place a few seeds on a damp paper towel and keep them in a warm area. If they sprout within a few days, the seeds are still good to plant. If not, it may be time to replace them.

For long-term storage, freezing is a good option, but it's critical that the seeds are completely dry before freezing to avoid damage. When ready to plant, thaw the seeds gradually to prevent shock from sudden temperature changes. It's also a good practice to rotate your seed stock regularly, using older seeds first and replenishing with freshly harvested ones. Keep in mind that different types of seeds have varying shelf lives. For example, tomato seeds can last up to five years, while onion seeds may only remain viable for one or two years under optimal conditions.

Composting

Composting is a natural process that turns organic waste into nutrient-rich material, perfect for improving your soil's health and reducing waste. To start, choose the method of composting that suits your space and needs. A compost bin works well for small areas like backyards or urban gardens, keeping everything contained. If you have more space, you can simply create a compost pile directly on the ground. For those who want to speed up the process, a compost tumbler is an excellent option, as it allows you to rotate the compost regularly.

Next, gather the Materials for composting, which include a mix of "greens" and "browns." Greens provide nitrogen and include kitchen scraps such as fruit and vegetable peelings, coffee grounds, and grass clippings. Browns, on the other hand, provide carbon and come from materials like dried leaves, straw, and wood chips. Both components are necessary for a balanced compost. The general guideline is to aim for a 3:1 ratio, with more browns than greens to maintain structure and airflow in the compost.

Once you have your materials, build your compost by alternating layers of browns and greens. Start with a layer of browns at the bottom to ensure proper airflow, then add a layer of greens. Continue this pattern until all materials are added. It's important to cover kitchen scraps with browns to reduce odor and deter pests. Breaking down large pieces of material helps speed up the decomposition process.

To keep the compost working efficiently, you'll need to turn or mix it every few weeks. This introduces oxygen into the pile, which is necessary for the microorganisms that break down the organic material. If you're using a compost tumbler, simply rotate it regularly. If not, use a shovel or pitchfork to turn the pile manually.

The compost should maintain a moisture level similar to that of a wrung-out sponge. Too much moisture can cause the pile to become soggy and smelly, while too little moisture will slow down decomposition. If the compost is too dry, add water. If it's too wet, balance it by adding more browns. Covering the compost pile with a tarp can also help regulate moisture levels, especially in dry climates.

Over time, you'll begin to see progress as the organic materials break down. The composting process can take anywhere from a few months to a year, depending on the materials used and how often the compost is turned. You'll know the compost is ready when it becomes dark, crumbly, and has an earthy smell. At this point, the original materials should no longer be recognizable.

Once the compost is fully decomposed, it can be harvested and used in your garden. Simply sift through the pile or empty your bin, and you'll have nutrient-rich compost ready to be added to garden beds, mixed into potting soil, or spread over your lawn.

To ensure success, avoid adding materials like meat, dairy, or oily foods, as these can attract pests and produce unpleasant odors. Also, steer clear of adding weeds or diseased plants, as they may spread when you use the compost. Items like eggshells and coffee grounds are great additions, providing valuable nutrients like calcium and nitrogen.

How to Deter Pests from your Garden

Keeping pests away from your garden can be challenging, but with the right strategies, you can protect your plants without relying on harsh chemicals. Here are some effective tips to deter pests naturally:

1. Encourage Beneficial Insects: Not all insects are bad for your garden. Ladybugs, lacewings, and predatory wasps help control harmful pest populations. You can attract these beneficial insects by planting flowers like marigolds, dill, and sunflowers, which provide nectar and habitat.

2. Use Companion Planting: Certain plants repel pests when planted near your crops. For example, planting marigolds around vegetables helps deter aphids, while basil and garlic can ward off mosquitoes and other insects. Companion planting can also enhance plant growth and improve yields.

3. Install Physical Barriers: Simple barriers can keep pests from reaching your plants. Use row covers, fine mesh netting, or floating covers to protect plants from insects like cabbage worms and squash bugs. You can also place collars made from cardboard or plastic around the base of plants to deter cutworms and slugs.

4. Maintain Healthy Soil: Healthy plants are more resistant to pests and diseases, so keep your soil nutrient-rich with compost or organic matter. Well-nourished plants will have stronger defenses against insects and other threats. Regularly aerating the soil and ensuring proper drainage can also help reduce pest problems.

5. Remove Weeds and Debris: Weeds and plant debris provide shelter for pests. Keep your garden tidy by pulling weeds regularly and cleaning up dead leaves, fallen fruit, or plant clippings. This helps reduce hiding places for insects like beetles, slugs, and snails.

6. Use Natural Predators: Introduce natural predators like birds, frogs, and toads into your garden to help control pests. Installing birdhouses or small ponds can attract these helpful creatures, which will feed on insects like caterpillars and beetles.

7. Handpick Pests: For smaller gardens, manually removing pests can be effective. Simply check your plants daily and remove pests like beetles, caterpillars, and slugs by hand. Dispose of them in a bucket of soapy water to prevent them from returning.

8. Use Organic Pesticides: If you need to resort to pesticides, opt for organic options like neem oil, insecticidal soap, or diatomaceous earth. These products can help control pest populations without harming beneficial insects or pollinators. Use them sparingly and follow the instructions carefully.

9. Crop Rotation: Changing the location of your plants each season prevents pests from building up in one area. Certain pests are attracted to specific crops, so rotating plant types in your garden can break their life cycle and reduce infestations.

10. Mulch Wisely: Mulching helps retain moisture and regulate soil temperature, but it also creates a habitat for pests like slugs if applied too heavily. Use mulch sparingly and choose materials like straw or wood chips that decompose slowly, reducing the likelihood of pests taking shelter underneath.

11. Water in the Morning: Water your garden early in the day so the plants dry off before evening. Moist conditions at night can attract pests like slugs, snails, and fungi. Wet leaves and soil also make plants more vulnerable to damage and disease.

12. Planting deer-resistant plants around the perimeter of your garden can help create a natural barrier. Deer tend to avoid plants with strong scents, rough textures, or thorny leaves. Some good options include:

- Lavender
- Rosemary
- Marigolds
- Mint
- Yarrow
- Russian sage

These plants can help mask the scent of your more appealing crops, making the garden less attractive to deer.

13. These natural, non-toxic deterrents can help keep slugs at bay.

- **Coffee grounds**: Sprinkle used coffee grounds around plants. The caffeine in coffee repels slugs, and they dislike the rough texture.
- **Epsom salts**: Some gardeners find success using Epsom salts around the base of plants. The salt irritates the slugs' bodies and discourages them from crossing.

- **Garlic spray**: Make a garlic spray by steeping crushed garlic in water overnight. Spray this mixture on your plants to repel slugs.

14. Rabbits tend to avoid plants with strong scents or bitter tastes. Surround your garden with plants that repel rabbits, creating a natural barrier. Some effective options include:

- Lavender
- Marigolds
- Sage
- Mint
- Onions
- Garlic

15. Natural repellents can help discourage rabbits from venturing into your garden. You can use commercial rabbit repellents or make your own at home. A mixture of garlic, hot peppers, and water sprayed around the garden can deter rabbits. Alternatively, sprinkle blood meal, bone meal, or human hair around the perimeter of your garden—rabbits dislike these smells and will often stay away. Reapply repellents regularly, especially after rain, to maintain effectiveness.

CHAPTER 10

NUCLEAR THREATS

Nuclear warfare is a threat that many people today have never had to seriously consider, but it's a danger we must be prepared for. During the Cold War, knowing how to respond to a nuclear disaster was common knowledge, but today, most people are unaware of what to do if the unthinkable happens. In the event of a nuclear explosion, it's not the fireball that causes the most destruction and death—it's the shockwave that follows. The fireball itself has a relatively small radius, but the shockwave can travel far and wide, wreaking havoc in its path.

Imagine this: you're outside or near a window, and suddenly, you see an incredibly bright flash—like staring directly into the sun. Whatever you do, don't try to locate the source of the flash. You have maybe 8-10 seconds to act if you're far enough away from the fireball. Immediately drop to the ground, face down, and cover your ears with your thumbs and your eyes with your fingers. Breathe through your teeth. Laying flat will help the shockwave pass over you, minimizing the risk of fatal injuries. If you remain standing, the force of the shockwave could cause your lungs, eardrums, and other organs to rupture.

Once the shockwave has passed, your next move is crucial—find shelter immediately. While the shockwave causes immense damage, the real danger comes from the nuclear fallout that follows. Don't attempt to travel; instead, get underground or find shelter in the nearest sturdy building. If you're near a stranger's house or a business, don't hesitate—get inside and put as much concrete and steel between you and the outside as possible.

The next 48 hours are critical. You must stay sheltered during this time, as the radioactive material from the fallout decays exponentially. Even if you survive the initial blast, venturing outside for even 20 minutes could expose you to lethal levels of radiation. After 48 hours, the radiation levels will have decreased significantly, and it will be safer to begin searching for your loved ones and leaving the city. Remember, patience and caution are your best allies in this situation. If you rush, you won't survive to reunite with your family or find safety. Take these precautions seriously—your life depends on it.

In the event of a nuclear attack, every second counts, and knowing exactly what to do can be the difference between life and death. Here's a comprehensive guide on how to respond effectively to maximize your chances of survival.

Recognize the Warning Signs

- Bright Flash: A nuclear explosion is often preceded by an intensely bright flash, brighter than the sun. If you see this, do not look directly at the source. The flash can cause temporary blindness or even permanent eye damage.
- Emergency Alerts: Pay close attention to emergency broadcasts, sirens, or alerts on your phone, radio, or TV. These systems may give you precious moments to prepare before the shockwave hits.
- Take Immediate Cover
- Indoors: If you're inside when the attack occurs, stay there. The best protection is deep inside a building, away from windows, with as many walls as possible between you and the exterior.
- Outdoors: If you're outside and witness the flash, drop to the ground immediately, face down, and cover your head. Lay flat to allow the shockwave to pass over you and reduce the risk of severe injury.

Protect Your Body

- Cover Your Eyes and Ears: Use your thumbs to cover your ears and your fingers to shield your eyes. This simple action helps protect against the blinding light and deafening noise of the explosion.
- Breathe Through Your Teeth: Breathing through clenched teeth can help protect your lungs from overpressure caused by the shockwave.

Seek the Best Shelter Available

- Underground Shelters: If possible, head to a basement or fallout shelter. The deeper and more shielded you are, the better your protection against radiation and fallout.
- No Basement? If you can't get underground, find the most central location in a sturdy building. Avoid exterior walls, doors, and windows.

Stay Sheltered

- 48-Hour Rule: Radioactive fallout from a nuclear explosion is most dangerous in the first 48 hours. It's crucial to stay sheltered during this time to avoid exposure to lethal radiation. The fallout decays exponentially, so waiting out these critical hours can significantly reduce your risk.

Decontaminate If Exposed

- Remove Contaminated Clothing: If you were outside during or after the explosion, remove your outer clothing as soon as possible. This can eliminate up to 90% of radioactive material on your body.
- Wash Thoroughly: Shower with soap and water as soon as possible to remove any remaining fallout particles. Avoid using conditioner, as it can bind radioactive particles to your hair, making them harder to remove. Use warm water and soap to scrub all exposed skin areas, paying special attention to hands, face, and hair. The friction from scrubbing is essential to dislodge radioactive particles. It's often recommended to wash multiple times to ensure as much radioactive material as possible is removed.

Prepare for an Extended Stay

- Supplies: Rely on whatever food, water, and supplies you've stored. Do not consume anything that may have been exposed to fallout. Your shelter should be stocked with enough essentials to last at least a few days.
- Seal Off Entry Points: Close off windows, doors, and any other points of entry to minimize the amount of radioactive dust entering your shelter. Duct tape and plastic sheeting can be helpful here.

Stay Informed

- Listen to Official Updates: Use a battery-powered or hand-crank radio to stay informed. Authorities will provide crucial information on when it's safe to leave your shelter and where to find help.
- Plan Your Next Steps
- Evacuation: After 48 hours, assess the situation based on official guidance. If it's safe, prepare to evacuate. Cover your mouth and nose with a mask or cloth to avoid inhaling any lingering radioactive particles.
- Reunite with Loved Ones: If separated from family, use this time in shelter to plan your reunion. Have a clear, safe meeting point established.
- Mental and Emotional Well-Being
- Stay Calm: Remaining calm under pressure is vital. Panic can lead to poor decisions; keeping your composure will help you think clearly and act efficiently.
- Support Each Other: If you're not alone, lean on each other for emotional support. Keeping spirits high can significantly impact your ability to cope and survive.

Surviving a nuclear attack isn't just about knowing what to do; it's about being mentally and physically prepared to act swiftly. Understanding where to seek shelter, how to protect yourself, and what steps to take afterward can save your life and the lives of those around you. While the thought of a nuclear attack is terrifying, having a plan in place can make all the difference. Stay informed, stay prepared, and always have a strategy for the unexpected.

In the event of a nuclear attack, protecting yourself from radioactive particles in the air becomes a top priority, and the right mask can make all the difference. Here's a rundown of the best options to keep you safe when it matters most:

PAPR (Powered Air-Purifying Respirator)

- Why It's Effective: A PAPR is like having your own portable air purification system. It uses a battery-powered blower to pull air through high-efficiency filters, providing you with clean, breathable air even in the most hazardous conditions. This mask offers exceptional protection against radioactive particles, as well as chemical and biological threats.
- Pros: Offers the highest level of filtration, provides positive airflow which makes breathing easier, and protects against a wide range of contaminants.
- Cons: It's a bit bulky, expensive, and requires batteries to function, so it's not the most convenient for everyone.

Full-Face Gas Mask with NBC (Nuclear, Biological, Chemical) Filter

- Why It's Effective: Designed to shield you from nuclear, biological, and chemical threats, this mask covers your entire face, including your eyes, offering comprehensive protection. With the right NBC filter, it effectively blocks radioactive particles, making it a solid choice in a nuclear scenario.
- Pros: Provides full-face coverage, comes in various models, and is relatively accessible compared to more advanced options.
- Cons: Can be uncomfortable to wear for extended periods, requires a perfect seal for effectiveness, and filters need to be replaced regularly.

N95 or N100 Respirators

- Why It's Effective: While these aren't specifically designed for nuclear fallout, N95 and N100 respirators can still filter out a significant portion of airborne radioactive particles. The N95 blocks at least 95% of particles, while the N100 offers even higher protection, filtering out 99.97%.
- Pros: Widely available, affordable, and simple to use.
- Cons: Doesn't protect your eyes, offers less protection compared to specialized masks, and may not filter out all radioactive particles effectively.

Military-Grade CBRN Masks

- Why It's Effective: If you want top-tier protection, military-grade CBRN (Chemical, Biological, Radiological, and Nuclear) masks are the way to go. These are designed for use in the most dangerous environments, offering excellent defense against radioactive particles and other hazardous substances.
- Pros: Provides the highest level of protection with filters specifically designed for nuclear fallout, and often includes built-in eye protection.
- Cons: They're pricey, require proper training to use effectively, and you'll need to replace the filters regularly.

DIY Improvised Mask

- Why It's Effective: If you're caught without a commercial mask, a makeshift mask using multiple layers of cloth or a damp cloth over your mouth and nose can offer some degree of protection against larger radioactive particles.

- Pros: You can make it quickly from readily available materials.
- Cons: Offers minimal protection, doesn't filter out smaller particles effectively, and doesn't protect your eyes.

No matter which mask you choose, a proper fit and seal are critical for it to be effective. Remember, your mask is just one part of your defense strategy—pair it with seeking proper shelter, decontaminating exposed skin and clothing, and minimizing time spent outside. The right mask, combined with smart actions, can significantly boost your chances of staying safe in a nuclear event. Stay prepared and stay safe.

CHAPTER 11

COMMUNICATION WHEN CRISIS ARISE

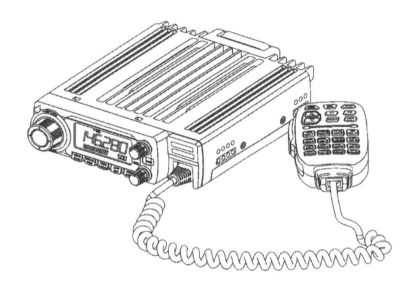

Walkie Talkies for the Family

A two-way radio is one of those tools that proves its value when you need it most, offering a level of communication that cell phones simply can't match in certain situations. When disaster strikes—whether it's a natural disaster, a power outage, or even just a camping trip in the wilderness—cell service can be spotty or nonexistent. That's where a two-way radio comes in, ensuring you stay connected no matter where you are. Unlike phones, they don't rely on fragile cellular networks that can fail at the worst possible time. You can trust that when you press that button, your message will get through.

One of the best things about two-way radios is their simplicity. No dialing, no waiting for a signal—just instant communication with a push of a button. When you're in a fast-paced or high-stress situation, this immediate connection is crucial. Whether you're coordinating with your family during a storm or staying in touch with your hiking group deep in the woods, the ability to communicate instantly could be a lifesaver.

Beyond that, two-way radios offer an added layer of security. You can set your radio to specific channels or frequencies, ensuring that only your group is in the loop. This is especially valuable in emergencies or crowded areas where other groups might also be using radios. Your communication stays clear, private, and uninterrupted.

And let's not forget about their durability. Two-way radios are built to withstand tough conditions, whether you're battling the elements outdoors or navigating a chaotic situation. Many models are designed with weather alerts, long battery life, and even water resistance, making them reliable in just about any circumstance you throw at them.

In short, having a two-way radio isn't just a convenience—it's a reliable, quick, and secure way to stay connected when it truly counts. Whether you're prepping for emergencies, enjoying the great outdoors, or just ensuring smooth communication in a tricky situation, a two-way radio is a must-have tool that delivers when you need it most.

Ham Radios

Ham radios, also known as amateur radios, are an exciting and powerful way to communicate, allowing you to connect with people across the street or across the world—without relying on the internet, cell towers, or any modern communication networks. This makes ham radios incredibly useful when other systems go down, like during natural disasters, power outages, or in remote areas where your phone might not get a signal. In short, it's your direct line to the world when all else fails.

Ham radio operators, or "hams," are part of a unique and passionate community. They can transmit and receive signals on a variety of frequencies using voice, text, or even digital data, with some operators chatting across continents or experimenting with sending messages through satellites. Whether you have a simple handheld radio or a full-blown home station with a high-powered antenna, ham radios are versatile and built to adapt to almost any situation.

One of the most compelling reasons people turn to ham radios is their critical role in emergencies. When traditional communication networks go dark, ham radio operators are often the ones stepping up, relaying vital information, coordinating rescue efforts, or just helping people stay in touch with loved ones. In fact, many emergency response teams rely on ham operators as a crucial backup system, knowing that they can keep communications flowing when it matters most.

But ham radio isn't just about emergencies—it's also a vibrant hobby with a global community behind it. Hams love experimenting, from building their own equipment to participating in global contests where they compete to make as many contacts as possible. Whether you're interested in learning new tech skills, diving into radio frequencies, or simply connecting with people around the world, ham radio has something for everyone.

Before you can get started, though, you'll need a license. Don't worry—it's part of the fun! The entry-level Technician license exam covers basic electronics, radio theory, and FCC regulations. Once you're licensed, you'll have access to a whole new world of local and regional communications. As you move up to higher levels, like the General or Amateur Extra licenses, you can unlock the ability to communicate internationally and explore more advanced frequencies.

Ham radio is more than just a communication tool—it's an adventure. Whether you're prepping for emergencies, eager to learn something new, or excited to connect with a worldwide community, ham radio opens up a world of possibilities. With just a radio in your hands, you can bridge gaps, solve problems, and be part of something much bigger.

CHAPTER 12

TIPS, TRICKS, AND RECIPES

Unfortunately, yeast has a short shelf life, which could make baking risen bread hard in trying times. This is how to make bread yeast with the natural yeast found on the skin of apples.

Apple yeast water:

Cut up a whole apple and cover with water in mason jar. **Warning: Do not create an air-tight seal. Doing so could cause the glass to crack or worse, a messy explosion from the gas buildup. Best to cover with cloth and secure with a rubber band to allow gasses to escape on their own or only place lid on the jar and leave the ring off completely.**

After 24 hours you should see tiny bubbles rising to the surface, which tells you that the yeast has been activated. Let sit for three days.

On day three, there should be larger bubbles at the top. Strain the apples from the yeast water and discard. Mix the yeast water with a cup of flour and add a tablespoon of sugar. It should be the consistency of pancake batter without lumps.

Store mixture into a larger mason jar, only filling 1/3 way, and let rest for 12 hours. The mixture should foam and rise, doubling in size. **Warning: Do not create and air-tight seal.**

Add a ½ c of the mixture to two cups of flour (white or wheat) and ½ c of water. Kneed into a ball and allow to rise for two hours in a bowl or until the dough doubles in size.

Preheat your oven at 425 F

Place dough round in the preheated oven and lower the temperature to 375 F. Bake until loaf is golden-brown, and the bottom is hollow sounding when you tap it.

In a doomsday scenario where conventional, electric ovens are unusable, place within parchment paper inside a Dutch oven, cover, and place over a bed of coals in your fire pit. Don't forget to add hot coals to the top of your covered Dutch oven so your bread evenly cooks.

- See directions for building your own clay/mud oven on page 104

Doomsday Crackers: Also called survival crackers, hardtack, or ship's biscuits.

   2 cups cornmeal

   1 cup water

   2 teaspoons salt

   Add spices optional

Mix the ingredients thoroughly, kneading the dough until everything is well combined.

Roll out the dough onto wax paper, then bake at 350 F until it turns a beautiful golden brown. Once the baked dough has the crisp consistency of crackers, let them cool completely.

Store your crackers in zip lock bags or any airtight container to keep them fresh.

Hard Tack: Simple and long-lasting, this type of bread that's been used as a staple for sailors, soldiers, and adventurers for centuries.

   2 cups all-purpose flour

   1/2 to 3/4 cup water

   1/2 teaspoon salt (optional)

   Preheat your oven to 375°F

In a large bowl, combine the flour and salt. Gradually add water while mixing until a stiff dough forms. The dough should not be sticky but should hold together.

Turn the dough out onto a floured surface and knead it for about 5-10 minutes until smooth. This helps to ensure the dough is well-mixed and workable.

Roll the dough out to about 1/4 inch thick. It's important that the dough is evenly rolled to ensure even baking.

Cut the dough into squares or rectangles. The size can vary, but traditionally, each piece is about 3x3 inches

Using a fork, poke holes in each square. This helps prevent the bread from puffing up during baking and allows it to dry out more thoroughly, which is key to its long shelf life.

Place the pieces on an ungreased baking sheet. Bake for 30 minutes, then flip the pieces and bake for an additional 30 minutes. The hard tack should be a light golden color and very hard.

Let the hard tack cool completely on a wire rack. Once cooled, store it in an airtight container. Properly stored, hard tack can last for years.

The harder and drier the hard tack, the longer it will last. You can add more or less water depending on the humidity of your environment and the type of flour you're using. If you want to make it more flavorful, you can add herbs or spices, but traditional hard tack is made with just flour, water, and sometimes salt. Soak in water, soup, or coffee to soften it before eating.

No knife or opener for your tuna can? No problem.

Rub the top of the can on a concrete surface vigorously, and you'll grind the lip of the lid right off. Then, with a quick squeeze on the sides, watch the lid pop open. If you're feeling extra resourceful, you can even create a dent in the center and bend the can to pop it open with your bare hands. It's a simple trick that'll make you feel like a survival pro.

Kindling and Candle Alternatives

Need to start a fire quickly and no dry kindling in sight? Chips (yes, the kind that go with dip) are some of the best fire starters you can find in a pinch. Very flammable and quick to ignite, you'll soon be will on your way to a larger fire in no time.

Run twigs through a pencil sharpener to make tinder

Save your dryer lint as an excellent fire-starting material. For even better results, coat it in petroleum jelly and pack it into an empty toilet paper tube. Store these homemade fire starters in zip-lock bags, and you'll have reliable, ready-to-use tinder in your bug-out bag whenever you need it.

Alcohol swabs are also a good alternative to kindling.

Out of candles? Place a makeshift wick like a popsicle stick in a glob of Crisco. A full tub Crisco candle could last up to a month.

A crayon will burn for an 15 minutes, so if you have a box of 96 crayons, you'll have light for 24 hours.

Ramen noodles are the ultimate survival hack. Not only are they a lightweight, go-anywhere pack food, but they can also double as a makeshift cooking stove in a pinch. Just soak that dried brick of ramen in a flammable liquid, and watch it ignite like a solid fuel puck, burning for up to 20 minutes per side. It's an unexpected, yet awesome way to cook or stay warm when you're out in the wild.

All you need is a piece of steel wool and a 9V battery, and you've got an instant fire starter. Just touch the battery terminal with the steel wool, and watch as sparks fly, igniting a blaze in seconds. For an even quicker flame, throw in some cotton balls to help the fire spread faster. It's a thrilling and super effective way to get a fire going in no time.

Terra Cotta Space Heaters

When the power's out and there's no electric heat, keeping warm becomes a top priority. Sure, lighting a fire in the living room might sound cozy, but without a fireplace, it's definitely off the table. Luckily, there's a clever alternative that uses something you can easily find at any hardware or garden store: a terracotta pot.

Terracotta isn't just for plants—it's also a fantastic conductor of heat. Here's the trick: flip a terracotta pot upside down and place a few candles beneath it. As the candles burn, the pot absorbs the heat and then radiates it out into the room. You'd be surprised how much warmth this simple setup can generate.

Just don't forget to set it on top of a couple bricks for the flame to breathe.

Place a few of these DIY heaters around and you'll be feeling nice and toasty in no time. It's an easy, resourceful way to stay warm when modern conveniences are out of reach.

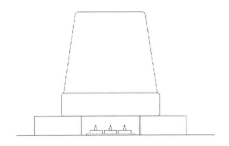

Collect Rainwater with a Tarp

When the rain starts to fall, don't let those precious drops go to waste. With just a large tarp and a 5-gallon bucket, you can turn a downpour—or even a light drizzle—into a reliable source of drinkable water.

Here's how it works: Spread the tarp out, securing the edges to create a slight funnel effect, and let it guide the rainwater straight into your bucket. In no time, you'll have a significant amount of fresh water collected, ready for use.

This simple survival trick is an easy way to harness nature's bounty, ensuring you stay hydrated when you need it most.

Bugs

When you're out in the wild and need a quick source of nutrition, bugs can be your best bet—especially when you know which ones to choose. In North America, there's a smorgasbord of edible insects that not only provide essential nutrients but are surprisingly high in protein. Here's a guide to some of the best bugs you can eat, along with how much protein they pack.

1. Crickets

- Protein Power: Around 12.9 grams per 100 grams. You'll often hear crickets before you see them, chirping away in grassy areas or near water. These little guys are a protein-packed snack that can be roasted, boiled, or even eaten raw if you're in a pinch.

2. Grasshoppers

- Protein Power: About 20.6 grams per 100 grams. These jumpers are common in fields, tall grass, and forests. Just be sure to remove their legs and wings before roasting or frying them for a crunchy, nutritious treat.

3. Mealworms (Larvae of Darkling Beetles)

- Protein Power: Roughly 18.7 grams per 100 grams. Look for mealworms in decaying wood or under rocks. These larvae can be roasted or fried and offer a satisfying crunch along with a protein boost.

4. Ants

- Protein Power: About 14 grams per 100 grams. These tiny powerhouses can be found under rocks and in anthills. Red and black ants are safe to eat and can be enjoyed raw or roasted for a tangy, zesty flavor.

5. Termites

- Protein Power: Around 13 grams per 100 grams. These wood-munchers are usually found in rotting trees or decaying wood. Termites can be eaten raw but roasting them gives them a more palatable taste.

6. Beetles (Various Species)

- Protein Power: Around 19 grams per 100 grams. Beetles are abundant under logs or in decaying matter. Their larvae, known as grubs, are particularly high in protein and can be roasted for a satisfying snack.

7. Cicadas

- Protein Power: About 9.6 grams per 100 grams. These noisy insects emerge from the ground, especially during their periodic cycles. Roast, boil, or fry them for a tasty, protein-rich meal.

8. Scorpions

- Protein Power: Approximately 13 grams per 100 grams. Scorpions are commonly found in desert areas. Roast or grill them, but don't forget to remove the stinger before chowing down.

9. June Bugs (Beetles)

- Protein Power: About 13.4 grams per 100 grams. These beetles are drawn to lights at night and can be found clinging to plants. Roast or boil them for a nutritious, crunchy snack.

10. Dragonflies

- Protein Power: About 12 grams per 100 grams. Skimming over ponds and lakes, dragonflies are quick but worth the effort to catch. Enjoy them roasted for a protein-rich snack.

Survival Tips:

- Cook It Up: Whenever possible, cook your insects to eliminate any parasites or bacteria. Roasting, boiling, or frying are your best bets.
- Avoid Bright Colors: Steer clear of brightly colored or foul-smelling insects, as they could be toxic. Stick to the safe options listed above.
- Ditch the Hard Parts: Remove wings, legs, and other hard bits to make your meal easier to digest.

Tips for Cooking:

- Roasting: Roasting insects brings out their natural flavors and gives them a crisp texture, making them a great topping or snack.
- Grinding: For a subtle addition, grind insects into a powder and mix them into flour, smoothies, or sauces.
- Seasoning: Don't forget to season. Spices, herbs, and sauces can complement the natural flavors of insects, making them even more delicious.
- With insects on your menu, you'll have a reliable source of protein to keep you fueled and focused in the wild. Who knew that survival could taste so good?

The Pros of Pellet Guns

Consider having a pellet gun on standby just in case the time comes when you may have to hunt small animals in your neighborhood.

Hunting small game with a pellet gun has several advantages:

1. Precision and Accuracy: Pellet guns are designed for high accuracy, allowing you to make precise shots. This is crucial when targeting small game, as a well-placed shot is necessary for a humane kill.

2. Reduced Noise: Pellet guns are much quieter than traditional firearms. This can prevent startling other animals in the area, providing you with multiple opportunities during a single outing.

3. Cost-Effective: Pellet guns and their ammunition are generally more affordable compared to traditional firearms and bullets. This makes it a cost-effective option.

4. Safety: Pellet guns have a lower risk of causing accidental injury or damage compared to high-powered rifles. The lower power and limited range make them safer to use in more populated areas.

5. Accessibility: In many regions, pellet guns have fewer regulations and restrictions than traditional firearms, making them easier to acquire.

6. Skill Development: Using a pellet gun requires and hones precise shooting skills, which can be beneficial for both beginner and experienced hunters looking to improve their marksmanship.

Overall, pellet guns provide an efficient, safe, and economical option for hunting small game, making them a popular choice among hunters.

Hunting small game with a pellet gun has several advantages:

1. Precision and Accuracy: Pellet guns are designed for high accuracy, allowing hunters to make precise shots. This is crucial when targeting small game, as a well-placed shot is necessary for a humane kill.

2. Reduced Noise: Pellet guns are much quieter than traditional firearms. This can prevent startling other animals in the area, providing hunters with multiple opportunities during a single outing.

3. Cost-Effective: Pellet guns and their ammunition are generally more affordable compared to traditional firearms and bullets. This makes it a cost-effective option for hunters.

4. Safety: Pellet guns have a lower risk of causing accidental injury or damage compared to high-powered rifles. The lower power and limited range make them safer to use in more populated or restricted areas.

5. Accessibility: In many regions, pellet guns have fewer regulations and restrictions than traditional firearms, making them easier to acquire and use.

6. Skill Development: Using a pellet gun requires and hones precise shooting skills, which can be beneficial for both beginner and experienced hunters looking to improve their marksmanship.

Shelters

Building a shelter in the wild isn't just a survival skill—it's your lifeline when the weather turns against you. Picture this: you're out in the wilderness, and the skies darken, the wind picks up, and you know a storm is coming. That's when your shelter becomes your best friend, offering a safe haven from the elements and keeping you warm and dry when it matters most.

First things first: location is key. You'll want to find a spot that's naturally protected from wind and rain, ideally with nearby resources like wood and water. Look around—are there natural features like rocks or dense foliage that could offer additional protection? Once you've got your spot, it's time to decide what kind of shelter suits your situation. Lean-tos, debris huts, and tarp shelters are all great options, each with its own set of materials and building techniques.

When gathering materials, think like nature. Branches, leaves, moss, and even grass can serve as excellent insulation, helping to keep the inside of your shelter cozy and waterproof. Remember, a well-insulated shelter is your best defense against the cold and damp.

Planning to build a fire inside your shelter? It's not just about warmth—it's about survival. But safety comes first. Make sure to clear the area of any flammable debris and ensure there's proper ventilation to avoid the risk of fire. Your shelter isn't just a roof over your head; it's your fortress, your warmth, and your refuge. Build it wisely, and it will serve you well.

A teepee shelter with branches is a practical and efficient sturdy, weather-resistant shelter in the wilderness. Here's a step-by-step guide to help you construct one:

Materials:
- Long, sturdy branches or poles (at least 8-12 feet long)
- Smaller branches or flexible sticks
- Cordage (rope, vines, or even strips of bark)
- Leafy branches, grass, pine boughs, or other insulating materials for covering

1. Choose a Location: Find a spot that's sheltered from the wind and away from any potential hazards like falling branches. Ideally, the location should be slightly elevated to avoid water pooling around your shelter.

2. Gather Materials: Collect long, straight branches for the frame. You'll need about 8-12 of these, depending on the size of your teepee. Also, gather smaller branches, leafy branches, or grass for covering and insulating the structure.

3. Create the Frame: Start by selecting three of the longest and sturdiest branches for the main support. These will form the tripod structure at the center of your teepee.

   - Form a Tripod: Arrange the three branches into a tripod shape, with the tops crossed over each other. Secure the crossing point tightly with cordage. This tripod will be the backbone of your teepee.
   - Add More Branches: Lean the remaining long branches against the tripod, spacing them evenly around the structure. Make sure the branches are angled to form a conical shape, with the tops meeting at the center. This will give your teepee its characteristic shape.

4. Secure the Frame: Once all the branches are in place, tie them together at the top with cordage to ensure stability. You can also tie some of the lower sections together for added support.

5. Cover the Structure: Begin layering smaller branches, leafy branches, or grass over the frame. Start from the bottom and work your way up, overlapping each layer like shingles. This will help shed rain and provide insulation.

- Insulate: To make your teepee warmer and more weather-resistant, add extra layers of leaves, moss, or grass. You can even use bark or pieces of cloth if available.

6. Leave a Ventilation Opening: It's essential to leave a small opening at the top of the teepee for ventilation, especially if you plan to have a fire inside. This opening will allow smoke to escape and fresh air to circulate.

7. Create an Entrance: Choose one side of the teepee to create an entrance. Leave a gap between the branches and reinforce it with additional branches or cordage to keep the structure stable.

8. Interior Setup: If you're planning to build a fire inside, clear a space in the center of the teepee and surround it with stones to contain the fire. Arrange the interior with bedding materials like leaves, grass, or blankets to make it more comfortable.

9. Test and Adjust: Once your teepee is built, take a step back and check for any gaps or weak points. Make adjustments as needed to ensure it is sturdy and weatherproof.

- Reinforce with More Materials: The more layers of natural materials you add, the better your teepee will insulate against cold and rain.
- Practice Fire Safety: If you light a fire inside, always have a way to extinguish it quickly, and never leave it unattended.

Simple Tarp Shelters

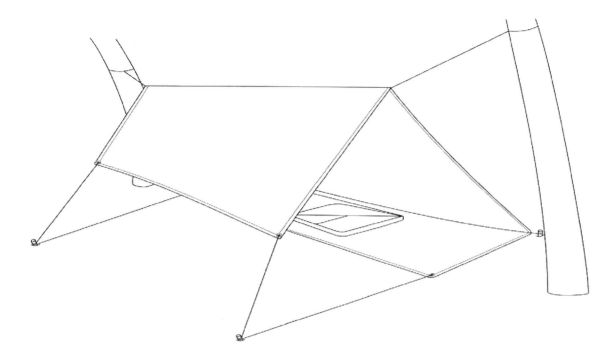

You can construct these shelter in just a few minutes. All you need is your tarp, paracord, stakes, and two sturdy trees, and you'll have a makeshift shelter to help keep you dry.

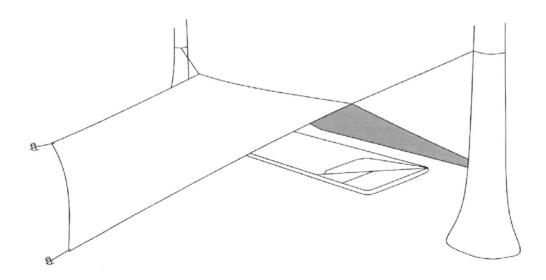

Signals

When you're lost, injured, or in need of help, signaling becomes your lifeline—the crucial connection between you and the rescuers who might be searching for you. In those moments, making sure you can be seen or heard is everything. Here's how to make sure your signal stands out and gets the attention it deserves.

Mirror: Flashing for Help

A mirror might seem like a simple tool, but in a survival situation, it can become your best friend. This small, reflective object can send a beam of sunlight miles away, catching the eye of a distant rescuer or pilot. If you've got a pocket-sized mirror in your survival kit, perfect. But don't worry if you don't—you can improvise with any reflective surface, like a piece of glass or metal.

To use it, hold the mirror close to your face, aiming the reflected sunlight at your hand first. Once you see that bright flash of light on your hand, you're ready. Move your hand away and angle the mirror towards where you think rescuers might be. A steady, well-aimed beam can reach far, but don't forget you can also create a flickering effect by tilting the mirror rapidly—this flashing light is like a visual shout, and it's hard to miss.

Whistle: Sound That Travels

In the wilderness, a whistle is more than just a loud noise—it's a beacon of hope that can carry over long distances, cutting through the silence or noise of the environment. Small, lightweight, and easy to carry, a whistle should be a permanent part of your gear. When you blow three sharp blasts, you're sending out the universal distress signal, a sound that rescuers will immediately recognize.

Unlike shouting, blowing a whistle takes less energy and won't strain your voice—a big plus if you're injured or exhausted. So, keep that whistle handy, and remember: three blasts, pause, repeat.

Fire: The Beacon of Survival

Fire is more than warmth and protection in the wild—it's also a powerful signal. A large, smoky fire in an open area is like a bright, waving flag that says, "Here I am." To make your fire more visible, add green leaves, wet grass, or other materials that produce thick smoke. During the day, the smoke will be visible from afar, while at night, the flames will light up the dark, guiding rescuers to you.

But you can take it a step further. Arrange the logs in your fire to form a distinctive pattern, like a triangle or an X—these shapes stand out and are easily recognized as signals of distress. You can also build three separate fires in a line or triangle, mirroring the three-blast whistle signal. Whether day or night, this method is a sure way to get noticed.

In a survival situation, every signal you send out is a message of hope. Whether it's the flash of a mirror, the piercing sound of a whistle, or the glow of a fire, make sure your signals are clear, visible, and impossible to ignore. Your life may depend on it.

Know your Knots

Mastering the art of knot tying isn't just a handy skill—it's a lifesaver in any survival situation. Whether you're rigging up a shelter, securing your gear, or fashioning a rescue line, knowing the right knot can make all the difference. Imagine the confidence of pulling a length of rope from your pack, ready to tackle whatever nature throws your way.

Here's a look at some essential knots that every outdoor enthusiast should know.

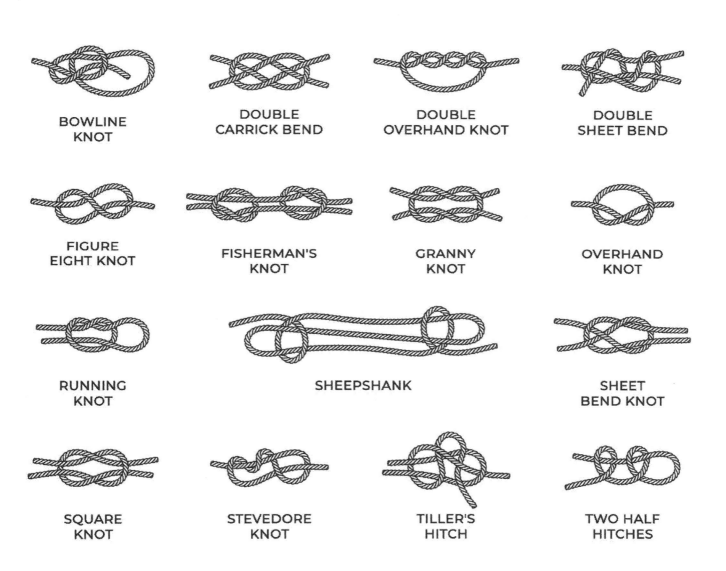

The Bowline: The Rescue Knot

The bowline is a must-know for creating a strong, secure loop that won't slip or jam, even under tension. This knot is perfect for rescue situations or when you need to anchor something safely. The beauty of the bowline is in its reliability—once tied, it holds fast, but when you need to untie it, it comes apart easily.

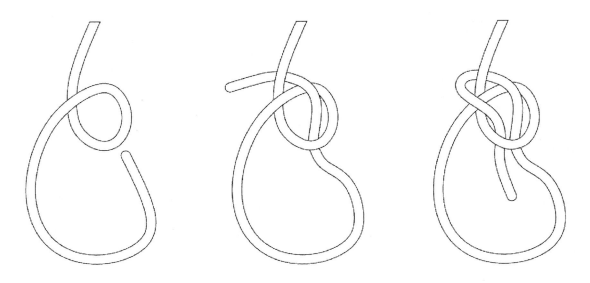

The Square Knot: The Binder

When you need to join two ropes of equal diameter, the square knot is your go-to. Simple and effective, it's perfect for binding things together—whether it's bundles of gear, securing a tarp, or tying off a bandage in a pinch. Just remember, the square knot is great for securing things that aren't under load but not for critical applications where lives depend on it.

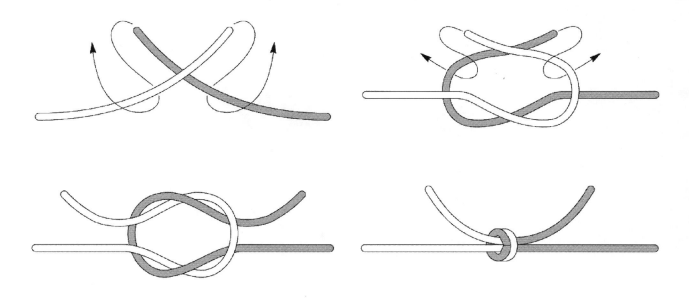

The Taut-Line Hitch: The Tension Adjuster

Setting up a tent or a tarp? The taut-line hitch is the knot you need. This adjustable knot holds tension well and allows you to easily tighten or loosen a guy line as needed. It's like having a built-in pulley system in your ropes, making campsite setup a breeze.

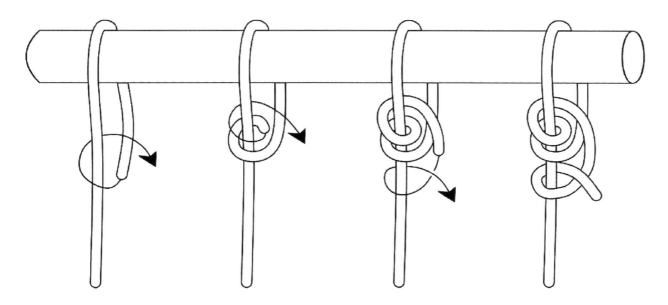

The Figure-Eight Knot: The Stopper

The figure-eight knot is your best bet when you need a strong stopper knot. It prevents the end of a rope from slipping through a pulley or a hole, and it's also the foundation for more complex climbing knots. It's a simple, yet powerful knot that should be in every survivalist's toolkit.

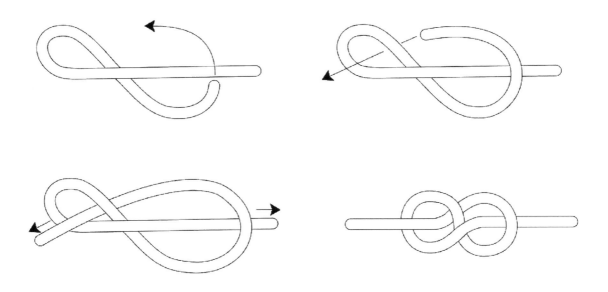

The Clove Hitch: Quick and Easy

The clove hitch is the knot you reach for when you need to secure a rope quickly around a post, tree, or another anchor. It's incredibly easy to tie and adjust, making it ideal for temporary tasks like setting up shelters or lashing gear together.

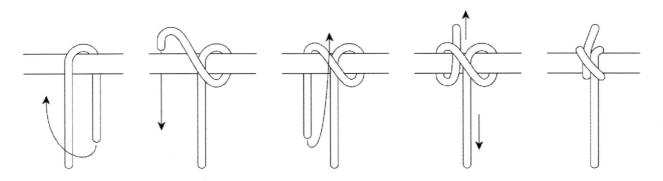

The Prusik Knot: The Climber's Friend

For those who might need to ascend or descend a rope, the prusik knot is indispensable. This friction knot grips the rope when weight is applied and slides easily when the weight is removed, making it perfect for creating a makeshift harness or for self-rescue in a climbing scenario.

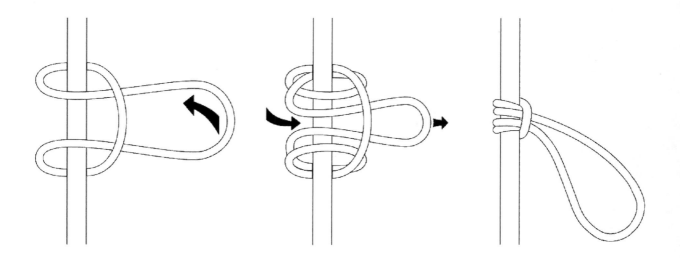

The Evenk Hitch: The Cold Weather Specialist

When dealing with cold weather or slippery rope, the Evenk hitch is your ally. It's particularly useful for tying off to trees or posts when you need a knot that won't freeze up or come undone in icy conditions.

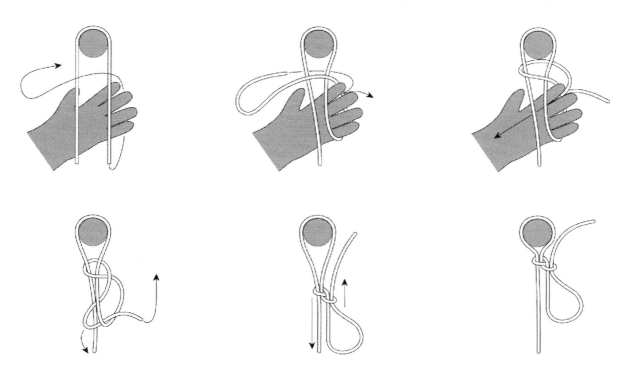

Practice Makes Perfect

Tying knots isn't just about knowing the steps; it's about muscle memory. Practice these knots until you can tie them in your sleep. In a survival situation, every second counts, and fumbling with a rope could cost you valuable time and energy. Always ensure your knots are tight and secure—loose knots can lead to accidents or failures at the worst possible moment.

The Square Lash

At some point, every Boy Scout learns the basics of lashings, but one of the most essential techniques to master is the Square Lashing. This versatile lashing is crucial for constructing sturdy structures like beds, chairs, ladders, and towers. Designed for strength, the Square Lashing is ideal for load-bearing joints, unlike the Diagonal Lashing, which is better suited for cross braces where maximum strength isn't necessary.

Ladder

By lashing smaller poles between two longer ones, you can quickly create a sturdy ladder. Whether you need to climb to new heights or construct taller structures, this simple technique is both effective and reliable.

Bed

Need a place to sleep? Take your ladder design up a notch by adding extra shorter poles—and maybe one down the center—to create a solid platform for a bed. While it's not something you'd sleep on directly, rolling out a sleeping pad and laying your sleeping bag on top will keep you off the ground for a more comfortable night's rest.

Stretcher

Dealing with injuries in the wild is no joke, especially when you're far from professional care. If someone gets hurt, moving them out of the area quickly is crucial. A stretcher, built similarly to the bed platform, can be the perfect solution for transporting an injured person over rough terrain. Just be mindful of the weight to keep it manageable.

Shelter

Need quick shelter? A simple lean-to can be constructed by square lashing several sticks together to form a wall. Cover this structure with leaves, bark, or a tarp, and you've got a reliable shelter to protect you from the elements.

Trap

If you've mastered the art of lashing, you can also create traps. A basic deep hole trap with a lashed top can keep prey contained, or you can construct a box trap if you're up for a challenge and have some extra time.

Camp Chair

Why sit on the ground when you can fashion a camp chair using square lashing? It's a simple, effective way to elevate your campsite comfort.

Meat pole

In the backcountry, keeping your food safe from animals is essential. Lash a long pole between two trees to create a meat pole, perfect for hanging your food or meat securely out of reach from critters like bears.

Knots and lashings might seem daunting at first, but they're built on simple, foundational techniques. By mastering just a few basic knots and lashing methods, like the square lashing, you can significantly boost your effectiveness in the wild. Whether you're aspiring to be a knot-tying expert or simply want to cover the basics, practicing these skills is a worthwhile investment in your outdoor abilities. Even a handful of reliable techniques can be game-changers in your survival toolkit. Keep in mind, not all knots are created equal—each has its unique strengths and is suited to specific tasks. Knowing when and how to use these knots is the key to mastering survival skills.

SQUARE LASHING

1. Start by tying a clove hitch not on the bottom side of the standing pole.

2. Begin your first wrapping.

3. Continue wrapping until there are three wrappings completed.

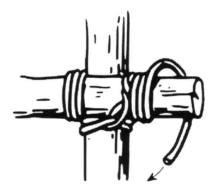

4. Prepare to begin the first frapping.

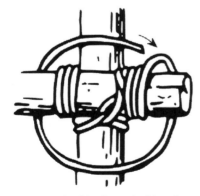

5. Complete the frist frap, cinching down on the existing wraps. Not the poles.

6. Complete three fraps and finish with a final clove hitch.

Crafting a Frog Gig

When you're out in the wilderness and hunger starts to set in, having the know-how to craft a simple but effective tool like a frog gig can make all the difference. This versatile, handmade spear isn't just for frogs—it can help you catch fish, small rodents, and other critters that might wander your way. Learning to make a frog gig from natural materials is a survival skill that can turn your outdoor experience from a struggle into a successful hunt.

First, you'll need to find a straight, sturdy sapling—something about 12 to 14 feet long is ideal. You want it to be long enough to reach your prey without getting too close, but still manageable to wield with precision. Once you've selected your sapling, carefully split the end into four sections. This will form the prongs of your gig. You can use a sharp rock or knife to make the split.

Now, here's where you start turning that sapling into a deadly hunting tool. Sharpen each of the four sections into a fine point. These prongs are what will pierce the skin and flesh of your prey, so take your time to make them as sharp as possible. Next, you'll need to create small wedges from wood or stone to insert between the points. These wedges help spread the prongs apart, increasing the chances of a successful catch by creating a wider striking area.

Once your frog gig is ready, it's time to put it to use. Unlike a spear that you throw, the frog gig is meant to be kept firmly in your hands. You'll use it to jab with precision and force at your target. The key here is stealth and patience. Slowly and quietly approach your prey—whether it's a frog perched on a rock or a fish hovering near the shore—and when you're close enough, strike with speed and strength.

Remember, the length of the prongs doesn't have to be exact, but they must be sharp enough to penetrate the tough skin and slippery flesh of your target. With practice, you'll get the hang of it, and soon enough, you'll be catching your dinner straight from the wild.

The frog gig is a testament to the power of simplicity. With just a few natural materials and some basic know-how, you can create a tool that significantly ups your chances of catching a meal. Whether you're in a survival situation or just enjoying a rustic day out in nature, this skill is one that will serve you well.

So, the next time you're in the great outdoors, give it a try. With your trusty frog gig in hand, you'll be ready to turn the wilderness into your dining room, one jab at a time. It's not just about survival; it's about mastering the art of living off the land and enjoying the bounty that nature provide.

Make a Fish Hook out of a Soda Tab

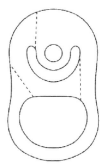 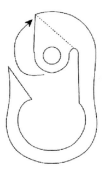 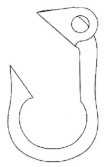

Gill Net: A Game-Changer for Survival Fishing

If hand fishing feels too hands-on, a gill net might be the perfect solution for your survival toolkit. This passive fishing technique allows you to set it and forget it, freeing you up to focus on other critical survival tasks while the net does the hard work for you.

A gill net works by snaring fish that swim into it. As fish attempt to pass through the net, they become trapped by their gills, making escape nearly impossible. It's a simple yet highly effective way to catch multiple fish without having to constantly monitor the water.

Creating a makeshift gill net is surprisingly straightforward if you have the right materials, such as monofilament line or strong cords. Stretch the net across a waterway—like a stream or along the edge of a river—and secure it well to ensure the current doesn't sweep it away.

The beauty of a gill net is its ability to work while you're busy elsewhere, making it an invaluable tool for ensuring a steady food supply in a survival situation. By incorporating a gill net into your survival gear, you significantly increase your chances of securing the sustenance you need.

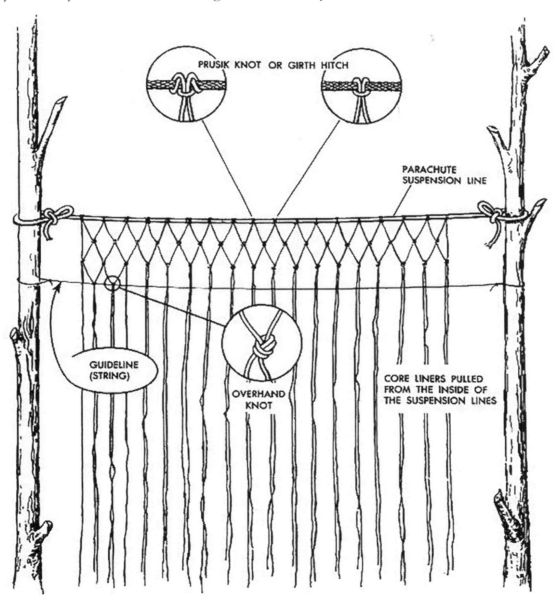

Create Cordage Out of a Two Liter Bottle

In recent years, a clever trend has emerged—upcycling those empty 2-liter soda bottles into something incredibly useful: durable strands of plastic. With a simple cutter, you can slice the bottles into strips of varying thickness, tailored to your specific needs. Whether you need thin, flexible strands or thicker, more robust ones, this method delivers.

These plastic strands are surprisingly strong on their own, but the real magic happens when you weave them together. By braiding or twisting the strands, you can create thicker, stronger cordage, perfect for a variety of survival or DIY projects. It's an ingenious way to turn trash into a valuable resource.

Making string from a soda bottle is a creative and practical way to recycle plastic and create durable cordage for various uses. Here's how you can do it:

Materials:

- Empty 2-liter soda bottle (or any plastic bottle)
- Sharp utility knife or scissors
- A straight edge or ruler
- A small cutting tool or jig (optional, but helpful for even strands)

Steps:

1. Prepare the Bottle:

- Start by cleaning the soda bottle thoroughly and removing any labels. Make sure the bottle is dry before you begin cutting.

2. Remove the Bottom and Top:

- Use a sharp utility knife or scissors to cut off the bottom of the bottle. Then, cut off the top portion, just below the neck. You should be left with a cylindrical piece of plastic.

3. Make the Initial Cut:

- Decide how thick you want your string to be. For thin string, make a narrow cut; for thicker cordage, cut a wider strip. Use a straight edge or ruler to guide your cut if you want to ensure consistency.
- Start by making a small incision at the edge of the bottle, creating a tab of plastic that you can grab onto.

4. Create the Continuous Strand:

- Once you have your starting tab, carefully begin pulling the plastic around the bottle in a spiral motion. As you pull, continue cutting along the bottle's edge, creating a continuous strip of plastic.
- For more uniformity, you can use a simple jig made from a piece of wood with a blade fixed to it, which allows you to guide the plastic through and cut even strips.

5. Lengthen the Strand:

- Continue cutting in a spiral until you've reached the end of the bottle. You should now have a long strip of plastic.

6. Strengthen the Cordage (Optional):

- If you need a stronger cord, you can braid or twist multiple strands together. Weaving or braiding them will create a thicker, more durable string that can be used for a variety of purposes.

7. Store or Use:

- Once you've created your string, you can wrap it around a spool or store it neatly for future use. This string can be used for tying, binding, or even crafting.

Tips:

- Adjust Thickness: You can experiment with different thicknesses of the strips to create the exact strength and flexibility you need.
- Use a Jig for Consistency: Creating a simple jig with a fixed blade can help produce more consistent strips, making the process easier and faster.

Materials:

Washers (stacked according to desired thickness of plastic wire

Two nuts

Two bolts

Wood board to stabilize

This method of making soda bottle string is not only a great way to recycle plastic but also provides you with a surprisingly strong and versatile cordage that can be useful in a variety of situations, from crafting to survival scenarios.

Bottle Cutting Jig

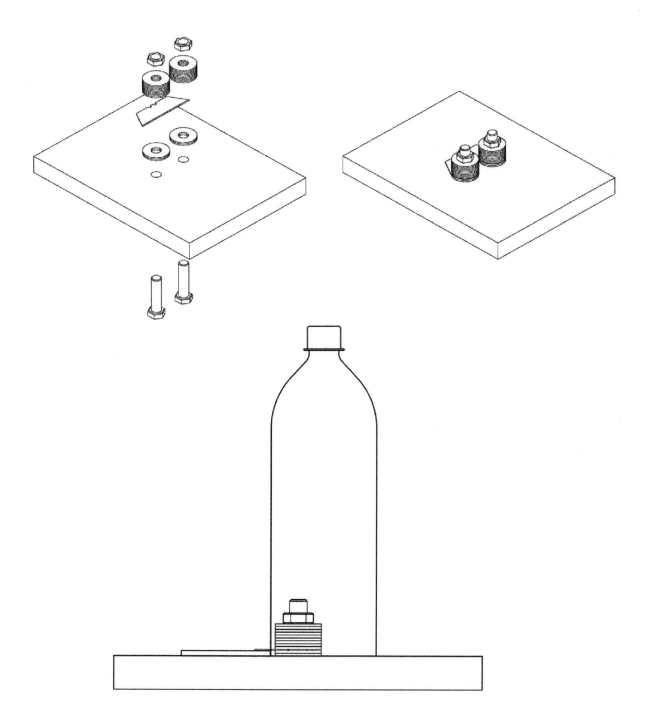

Made in the USA
Coppell, TX
14 December 2024

42507838R00081